the Show Makers

Great Directors

of the American

Musical Theatre

Lawrence
Thelen

routledge
new york • london

Published in paperback in 2002 by
Routledge
29 West 35th Street
New York, NY 10001

Published in Great Britain by
Routledge
11 New Fetter Lane
London EC4P 4EE

Printed in the United States of America on acid-free paper.

Thelen, Lawrence.
　　The show makers: great directors of the American musical theatre / by Lawrence Thelen.
　　p. cm.
　　Includes index.
　　ISBN 0-415-92346-8 (hb)
　　ISBN 0-415-92347-6 (pb)
　　1. Theatrical producers and directors—United States—Biography. 2. Musicals—
　　Production and direction. I. Title.
　　PN2285 .T48 1999
　　792.6'0233'092273—dc21
　　[B]

Archival Documentation
Interviews were held on the following dates: **Martin Charnin**, May 9, 1997, and May 23, 1998; **Graciela Daniele**, September 3, 1997, and October 2, 1998; **James Lapine**, May 6 and August 25, 1997; **Arthur Laurents**, May 6, 1997, and March 30, 1998; **Richard Maltby Jr.**, May 7, 1997, and April 15, 1998; **Des McAnuff**, May 26 and November 6, 1998; **Mike Ockrent**, May 6, 1997, May 20 and August 5, 1998; **Tom O'Horgan**, May 5, 1997, and May 19, 1998; **Harold Prince**, June 6 and August 28, 1997; **Jerome Robbins**, September 30, 1997; **George C. Wolfe**, September 4 and November 6, 1998; and **Jerry Zaks**, May 8, 1997, and April 17, 1998.

Photography Credits
Cover Photo (Jerome Robbins and Mary Martin during rehearsals of *Peter Pan*, 1954), Photofest; **Martin Charnin**, Courtesy of Martin Charnin; **Graciela Daniele**, Bruce Glikas, photographer/STQ Productions; **James Lapine**, Courtesy of James Lapine; **Arthur Laurents**, Photofest; **Richard Maltby Jr.**, Bruce Glikas, photographer/STQ Productions; **Des McAnuff**, Photofest; **Mike Ockrent**, Courtesy of Mike Ockrent; **Tom O'Horgan**, Courtesy of Tom O' Horgan; **Harold Prince**, Photofest; **Jerome Robbins**, Archive Photo; **George C. Wolfe**, Michal Daniel, photographer; **Jerry Zaks**, Courtesy of Russell Lehreh; Tony Walton, photographer.

the Show Makers

acknowledgments

First and foremost, I express gratitude to the directors featured in this book for their generosity, time, and philosophies. I also thank them for their encouragement and belief in the importance of a book of this nature. Thanks also go to the directors' assistants, who were often instrumental in organizing interviews and obtaining information. Furthermore, a handful of books proved invaluable to my work: Gerald Bordman's *American Musical Theatre: A Chronicle*, Ken Mandelbaum's *Not Since Carrie*, and Steven Suskin's *Opening Night on*

Broadway and *More Opening Nights on Broadway*. If one has not already benefited from these books, I encourage the reader to take full advantage of the tremendous work these authors have done in helping to bring the American musical theatre into focus. Gratitude for professional support, criticism, and advice are extended to Dr. Mark Zelinsky, Dr. Peter Levine, and my editor, William Germano. Additionally, thanks go to Patricia Roost for interview transcriptions; Robert Hatch for use of the camp; and Sylvia Jeanne Leibley (posthumously), Quentin "Boots" Thelen, Edith and Jim Lynch, and Michael and Marleen Thelen for their love and support. Finally, I thank Irene V. Hatch, whose help, encouragement, patience, low tolerance for procrastination, working knowledge of computers, and love (from the beginning of the journey to the end) put this book in your hands.

preface

This book is for anyone who loves the American musical, and specifically those who appreciate the craft and artistry involved in the creation of those musicals. It provides a rare opportunity to hear what some of the great directors of the musical theatre have to say about their craft and their careers. All the directors in the following chapters are and have been major forces in the American musical theatre, yet their approaches are profoundly different, their stories are unique and original, and their work habits are creative and distinct. Here, directors reveal how they

directed some of the most important, celebrated, and influential musicals of the twentieth century. Along with explaining how they function
in the musical theatre—their approach to collaboration, casting, staging,
and the like—the directors also share numerous anecdotes of their varied careers. Among them are Arthur Laurents's discovery and casting
of Barbra Streisand in her first Broadway show, *I Can Get It for You
Wholesale*; Jerome Robbins's integration of the "fiddler on the roof"
metaphor into his masterpiece; Harold Prince's reworking of *Cabaret*
following an influential Russian vacation; Tom O'Horgan's use of insect
imagery in *Jesus Christ Superstar*; Graciela Daniele's cutting of the best
song from *Once on This Island*; and many more. In addition, the book
contains Jerome Robbins's final interview.

These profiles offer a kind of seminar with great directors. Although
I have written them for anyone with a love of American musicals, those
readers who have an interest in how musicals actually work will also
find something of practical value here. For the student-director, these
in-depth chapters make up a sort of how-to book. However, nowhere in
the book does it say, "This is *how to* direct a musical." Instead, the
philosophies revealed within these pages are set forth for the reader's
perusal. By comparing and contrasting one chapter against the other
(one *director* against the other), the reader is able to make connections, find similarities and differences, gather suggestions, and thus
hone his or her own philosophy and understanding of the director's
role in the American musical theatre. By exploring and defining the
director's role, this book helps to delineate all the other job descriptions in the musical theatre. It should be noted that this is not a book
that chronicles how playwrights, composers, lyricists, actors, designers, or producers see the role of the director (and they may, in fact, see
it quite differently). The role of the director in the American musical
theatre is here explained by the directors themselves.

This book contains profiles of those directors from whom I could

obtain firsthand information. Certainly there are other influential directors of the twentieth-century American musical who are no longer with
us to explain how they worked: among them are George Abbott,
Michael Bennett, Gower Champion, Bob Fosse, and Rouben
Mamoulian. Although many of these directors are cited within these
chapters, giving us a glimpse of their greatness, I have not included individual chapters on these directors. It was not my intention to *speculate*
on these director's philosophies, influences, and approaches through
secondhand or incomplete accounts. Some suggested I include these
directors by presenting interviews with performers, designers, choreographers, and others who worked closely with these masters. However,
how someone else *perceives* a director's philosophy may not, in fact,
truly represent that director's own ideas, nor is anyone able to explain
and justify adequately a director's decisions from anything other than
an outsider's perspective. Without a doubt, it is a shame that extensive
interviews on the art of directing with these giants do not exist.
However, that should not diminish the importance of those that remain:
Martin Charnin, Graciela Daniele, James Lapine, Arthur Laurents,
Richard Maltby Jr., Des McAnuff, Mike Ockrent, Tom O'Horgan, Harold
Prince, Jerome Robbins, George C. Wolfe, and Jerry Zaks.

Not only are the directors in this book responsible for directing some
of the most important and influential musicals of the twentieth century,
but in doing so, they are literally directing the *future* of the American
musical. Through these directors' work, ambassadors of the American
musical (professional directors, civic/community directors, college professors, dedicated high school drama teachers) derive not only the
inspiration, but also the blueprints, to present and revive the Broadway
musical around the world. The changing of a line in Boston, the cutting
of a number in Hartford (whether well thought out to better develop the
story line, or hastily due to an actor's inability or a second act that is running too long) are directorial choices that become permanently docu-

mented in the published script, the original cast album, and the public-
ity photographs of the original cast. When director Rouben Mamoulian
turned over sections of the storytelling to choreographer Agnes de Mille
(with the help of Rodgers and Hammerstein), he was no longer simply
directing *Away We Go!*; he was *redirecting* the direction of the art form
itself. Today *Oklahoma!* (1943), which Mamoulian's show was later
renamed, stands as the pinnacle of influential musicals in the twentieth
century. However, whether in large strides, as with *Oklahoma!*, or in
smaller steps, the musical form constantly changes and grows. The
directors chronicled within this book are responsible for many of those
steps.

making the show

It is impossible to create a science out of an art form, and it is folly to believe that a set of directorial rules can be established that, if followed, will lead one to success on the musical stage. Indeed, directing musicals is a highly subjective and very personal experience. There are as many different ways to approach it as there are directors, and a number of different methods can lead to success. What works for one director may not necessarily be appropriate for another. Personality, influences, education, experience, and goals all have a significant impact upon the makeup of one's directorial philosophy. What some directors deem critical, other directors completely contradict or dismiss. Of course, more and varied philosophies beyond those included herein are certainly legitimate, and one is hard-pressed to find fault with a method if it ultimately leads to success on stage. However, a number of stylistic and philosophical similarities are present among these professionals—similarities that appear to have merit and value in defining the job description of the director of the musical. The following is a synthesis of the directors' philosophies.

There is no single approach that is appropriate for directing every musical. This sentiment is continuously voiced by nearly all the directors. What rehearsal techniques, points-of-view, and methods they used on one production either did not work or were not appropriate on the next. Almost all of the directors balk at trying to put concrete answers to abstract, artistic questions, noting that each project makes different demands, often requiring different solutions, even to similar problems experienced in previous shows. More often than not, directors cite the text as having the greatest influence over how they approach a particular show. Additionally, understanding the psychology of leading and working with people, knowing how to encourage and bring out individual excellence, and understanding and incorporating structure into the storytelling are seen, almost unanimously, as keys to the director's job.

Directors rarely begin their careers in the theatre as directors; instead they enter the theatrical world from other disciplines. Charnin and Maltby were both successful lyricists before turning to directing; Daniele and Robbins began as Broadway chorus dancers; O'Horgan and Zaks were performers; Laurents, McAnuff, and Wolfe started out as playwrights; and Prince came up through the ranks as stage manager and producer. Only Lapine and Ockrent actually began their professional careers in the theatre as directors. It could be argued, then, that having experience in other areas of the theatre besides directing gives the director a better perspective of the art form. Certainly, such experience allowed most of these directors to observe the process of mounting the Broadway musical from a vantage point within the system before taking over the reins themselves.

Not all of the directors attended college, and of those that did, many hold degrees in disciplines other than theatre. Some come from adjacent arts such as painting (Charnin), graphic design (Lapine), and music (O'Horgan), while others come from different disciplines entirely such as physics (Ockrent). A number of the directors hold master's degrees (Lapine, O'Horgan, Wolfe, and Zaks), while both director-choreographers (Daniele and Robbins) came up through the ranks of the professional dance world without any formal college training. Overall, most of the directors emphasize the importance of a solid general education beyond a mere theatrical education; this, they argue, provides the director with the widest breadth of knowledge upon which to draw. Although a number of them have had a close association with, and even taught courses at, colleges and universities, they are almost unanimous in their disapproval of the university system as a training ground for potential directors of the professional American musical theatre. Instead, a number of the directors point to the regional theatre system as providing that education for young directors.

Learning how to direct the musical is considered a hands-on experience by the directors, and they highlight two specific ways of doing this. The first is practical experience: through the actual mounting of musicals directors gain firsthand knowledge of the craft. Since many of the directors view the theatre as a type of apprentice system, it is not suprising that the second method most often suggested to student-directors is to work as a professional director's assistant. Performance experience is generally seen as having little impact on a director's work, and the ability to read music is almost unanimously regarded as unnecessary, even by those directors who do read music. Most agree, however, that a musical *understanding* is critical for the director of musicals.

When working on a new musical specifically, and at times when working on a revival, these directors generally prefer to be on board a project from the very beginning. This allows them to have influence over the structure of the show. To this end, both knowing structure and incorporating it when necessary while working in collaboration with the book writer, composer, and lyricist are among the director's most important functions. In contrast, being handed a musical after it has already been written leaves little room (and is often too late) for the director to act as a quality controller over the show's structure, ultimately making the job one of interpretation rather than creation. Although this is a valid job (often the primary one in a revival), it takes a backseat to these directors' desire to mount a show from an "authorial" point of view. Indeed, most view the director's job as inherently embodying the work of an author. Interestingly, nearly all of the directors featured in this book have at one time or another worked as writers in the theatre (if one considers both director-choreographers as writers through the creation of their dances). Although most of them acknowledge that they have at times gone into rehearsals without a completed script and score, a majority of them condemn the practice, citing it as an unnecessary risk that rarely results in success. Additionally, most of them believe that the director, and not the writers, should serve as the final editor of the script and score; the director must have the final say in order to bring about a consistent and unified production. Lapine, McAnuff and Ockrent, however, feel this final decision-making power should be shared with the musical's writers.

The directors who often serve as their own writers (Charnin, Lapine, Laurents, Maltby, and Wolfe) stress the importance of separating the distinct roles of writer and director if one is to be successful wearing both hats on a production. Only when a director can separate (though not necessarily divorce) the two roles can he or she be objective in assessing the show from a directorial point of view. Despite this challenge, most state a preference for directing their own work. It is not only the writer-director who prefers the duality of his or her job; most of the directors have held multiple positions on a single production: Charnin (lyricist-director); Daniele (choreographer-director); Lapine (writer-director); Laurents (writer-director); Maltby (lyricist-director); Ockrent (adaptor-director); Prince (producer-director); Robbins (choreographer-director); and Wolfe (writer-director and producer-director). Most admit this takes considerably more work; however, they willingly put forth the extra time required in exchange for the additional control it gives them over the production.

Ultimately, the directors define their job as that of the leader through which the entire production must be funneled. There must be one leading, driving, cohesive force, by which the entire production is assembled: that force is the director. This is not to say that they disregard collaboration. On the contrary, although each often has strong ideas about a show, none of them heads into a production assuming he or she has *all* the answers. To some degree each acknowledges dependence upon the creative ideas of their collaborators. Indeed, the more ideas offered and available, the greater the director's resources. Directors who allow others to contribute to their vision tend to develop more fully realized shows and performances. Despite that, they are often extremely discriminating about which ideas they will incorporate, or upon which they will choose to elaborate. The directors give their creative team and acting company a clear vision of how they see the production, then expect these artists to bring their experience and expertise to their particular jobs. Upon this foundation the collaborative process develops.

All of the directors believe collaboration is imperative, but that does not prevent many of them from wielding a firm hand when leading their productions. Daniele and O'Horgan see themselves as more permissive than dictatorial in their approach to the collaborative process; Lapine and Ockrent specifically refer to themselves as "collaborative," a term that can also be applied to Wolfe as he sees himself as both permissive and dictatorial "at the exact same time." However, half of the directors describe themselves as more dictatorial than permissive and believe, to some degree, this approach is necessary to bring about a unified production. Each notes, however, that being able to take such a strong hand in leading a production is only possible because of their in-depth and intimate knowledge of the material.

Most of the directors state that feeling passionate about their work is a prerequisite for effective directing, and they often use this as a basic criterion when choosing projects. The director who is passionate about his or her work not only gains more personally from the experience, but also often invests more of him- or herself into the work, which results in a higher quality of production. Young directors, however, should balance this passion for their work with the need to gain practical experience and should not overlook opportunities that serve to achieve this end.

The directors are split as to whether or not one should approach plays and musicals in the same manner. On one side are those who say they direct both similarly (Daniele, Lapine, O'Horgan, Prince, Robbins, Wolfe, and Zaks); on the other side are those who see the two genres as separate, even opposite forms (Charnin, Laurents, Maltby, McAnuff, and Ockrent). Ironically, the goals for each type of production are almost identical, so it seems the distinction is merely in how the directors approach the work. The difference appears to stem from how they perceive the storytelling qualities of the musical theatre. For example, Lapine and Laurents, although on opposite sides of the debate, both note that musicals require a different *style* of acting than straight plays. Does that style change, or is that style different, depending upon whether one approaches the genres similarly or differently? It seems unlikely; thus, the end result is the same even though the path to get there is different. A key aspect of the musical—its inherent theatricality, or "trappings"—seems to be the determining factor for a number of the directors. They recognize that these trappings are more prevalent in musicals than in straight plays, yet those that approach the two forms *differently* tend to utilize these trappings more judiciously, while those directors who approach the two forms *similarly* revel in them. It may well be that directors who approach both genres in a similar fashion sense a greater freedom to incorporate music and other theatricalities into their straight plays without feeling that they are making them into "musicals"; whereas directors who approach them differently may feel a self-imposed limitation to stay more closely to the text itself and refrain from including what might be perceived as the "trappings" of the musical theatre.

The obvious difference, of course, is that with a play the director is working primarily with one dramatist, the playwright; whereas, to paraphrase McAnuff, on a musical the dramatist is made up collectively of the composer, the lyricist, the book writer, the director, and at times the choreographer. In this way the function of the musical's director may be viewed differently—more of a "team leader" than a solo interpreter. The goal in terms of "telling a story that will transport an audience into a place that is hopefully religious," as Zaks says, whether through acting, singing, or dancing, remains the same regardless of the genre, however.

Half of the directors specifically point out the importance and benefits of research prior to and during pre-production. Research, they agree, builds up a reservoir of information from which to draw upon throughout the process. Once into pre-production, designing and casting (not necessarily in that order) are cited as the two most important areas on which the director must focus. While the scenic designs are frequently mentioned as being of primary concern, costume and lighting designs are also included. A number of the directors point out the importance of leaving some "flexibility" in the show's scenic design. This allows the scenic aspect of the show to continue to develop as the script does and also makes it easier, if necessary, to adapt quickly to unforeseen changes in the production once on stage.

Half of the directors rate casting as *the single most important job the director performs*. At the same time, they refer to the audition process as "gruesome," "ugly," "inhumane," "grisly," and "uncivilized." Unfortunately, none of the directors has yet been able to find or develop a viable alternative to the practice. Because of the opinion the directors have of the process, and their awareness of the negative effects it has on performers, the majority of them go out of their way to ease the discomfort. Most say that in auditions they do not look for one particular talent (acting, singing, or dancing) over another, but rather cast according to the demands of each role. Prince and Robbins go one step further by intimating that they look for performers who are innately similar to the characters they will play. A number of them admit to having on occasion miscast roles, often due to "flashy" auditions that fooled them into believing the performer had more talent and depth than he or she actually possessed. But all of them suggest that for the sake of the show a miscast actor should be replaced. Not only is the miscast actor detrimental to the quality of the production, but also, as Lapine and McAnuff both point out, it is a disservice to that actor to allow the person to present themselves in a role in which he or she cannot succeed. Obviously, in venues geared toward giving actors experience (community theatre productions, high school productions, and the like) good judgment must be used to balance the quest for a quality production with the need to educate actors. As far as stars are concerned, all of the directors acknowledge the potential box office appeal that casting a name star generates. However, half of them are quick to point out that stars should still be cast for their talent and appropriateness for the role, and not on their name alone.

Once rehearsals begin, a division among the directors appears. Some directors (Charnin, Maltby, McAnuff, Ockrent, Wolfe, and Zaks) believe that the company should sit around the table reading and analyzing the script. Others (Daniele, Lapine, Laurents, O'Horgan, Prince, and Robbins) believe in getting the company on their feet immediately and commencing with the staging. Certainly, taking time to study the script cannot hurt the show. What can be detrimental, however, is an exorbitant amount of time given to the process. The debate is largely divided between the "senior" and the "junior" generation of directors; the more senior directors choose to get the company on their feet at the outset. Also included in the group that start on their feet are the choreographers as well as O'Horgan, who often incorporates a great deal of movement into his productions. Generally, then, movement-oriented directors and those of the earlier generation tend to work from a more physical frame of reference, whereas the generation of directors coming of age after *Hair* (1968—the beginning of the concept-musical era) choose to study the script first. Lapine is the only one of the "junior" directors to cross over this line. It could be argued that with the depth in terms of subject matter and themes the musical form has taken in recent years, more analysis of present-day librettos is necessary; that is, "junior" generation directors are merely doing what the talents and hard work of the "senior" directors have forced them to do. Analyzing the high-concept script until the company feels "comfortable" with it may be a sensible compromise. And an original musical may require more analysis than the remounting of a fairly well-known work. Ultimately, however, the skill level of the company and the time the director has to mount the production will influence the amount of time spent on script analysis.

In terms of staging, McAnuff and Zaks are the only two who routinely pre-block their shows on paper ahead of time. Lapine and Maltby will at times pre-block a crowd scene or work out traffic patterns if work-ing with a stage full of actors, but they refrain from pre-blocking if a sequence is not particularly complicated. The majority of the directors, however, either refuse to pre-block, claiming it stifles creativity, or pre-fer to utilize the talents, imaginations, and instincts of their company and thus work out the staging with the actors' input. Whether prepared on paper ahead of time or not, almost all of the directors are open to the suggestions of their actors throughout the blocking process.

Is this a rule of thumb to be followed by all? Should all directors throw away their pencils, graph paper, and chessboards and abandon pre-blocking practices? If working at the professional level with profes-sional actors, this may indeed prove to be a more fruitful system. Certainly there are imaginative actors and directors at lower levels of the theatrical scale who can succeed in the context of an unstructured, creative collaboration. However, it should be noted that quality staging at the professional level often evolves from an in-depth understanding of a script, a scene, and its characters—an in-depthness that is almost second nature to a director after a year or two of pre-production work. Often college professors, community directors, and high school drama teachers lack this luxury of time. Heading into rehearsals without any preparation and "hoping" the staging will come together may not be an appropriate approach for all directors. Only through experimentation can each director determine the appropriate system for him- or herself. Ultimately, the level at which one is mounting the production should influence the director's need for preparation.

When it comes to musical staging, director-choreographers such as Daniele and Robbins stage their own musical numbers including the dances and ballets. O'Horgan is also known to do a good deal of his own musical staging. For the nondancing director, however, the rela-tionship between themselves and the choreographer is often a close, collaborative one. Although they will often stage their own ballads, duets, and, at times, comedy numbers, most directors work in collaboration with their choreographers on the musical staging, sharing the staging of many musical numbers. More often than not, however, when "steps" or "counts" are required, these directors tend to turn the work over entirely to the choreographer, while at the same time retaining the right to suggest changes and incorporate ideas.

All of the directors who have experience with out-of-town tryouts agree that these provide the best way to break in a show prior to opening on Broadway, for they give the production team an opportunity away from the harsh attention of the New York public and press to polish the production. Yet opening out of town is prohibitively expensive. And the current practice of previewing a show directly on Broadway is seen by most of the directors as an inadequate substitute. Workshop productions have thus become a place to polish before opening on Broadway, even though most of the directors view them as an unenjoyable step in the process. Overall, previews are looked upon as the next natural step in the rehearsal process and not as the beginning of the performance process. It is during this time that the theoretical ideas incorporated during pre-production and in rehearsals are seen in their practical context before an unbiased preview audience. Rehearsals do not cease once previews begin. All of the directors continue to hold daytime rehearsals during the preview period in which they incorporate solutions to problems recognized in performance. For many directors, being able to read and understand what the preview audience is communicating through their body language, attentiveness, and responses is critical to fine-tuning the production.

Once a show has officially opened, all of the directors recognize the importance of maintaining its quality. That is not to say, however, that they all go about it similarly. Most agree the best approach is to attend the show on a regular basis and give notes to the company. But attendance varies greatly from director to director: from "all the time"

(Maltby and Prince) to "every couple of weeks" (Lapine) to "every couple of months" (Daniele) to "occasionally" (Robbins). Even those directors who confess they do not enjoy going back and revisiting their work (Charnin, Robbins, and Wolfe) realize the importance of doing so for sustaining quality. Few directors take on this burden alone. Many of them utilize quality stage managers and trustworthy assistants (who are often endowed with the authority to give notes) to oversee productions, particularly if a director has multiple shows running simultaneously. Because casting stands out as the most important function the director performs, it is not surprising that almost all of the directors actively involve themselves in major cast replacements once a show is up and running. However, less than half of them say they alone rehearse new performers in their roles; it is most common among the directors to turn over the blocking rehearsals to a stage manager. Following that, the director will either work with the new performer directly prior to putting them into the show, or give notes to the new performer once they have begun performances.

Although none of the directors specifically sees a difference in his or her job description when directing a revival, almost all of them point out differences that emerge from a creative standpoint. Most agree there is no reason to approach a revival as a re-creation of the original production. A number of directors, including Laurents, O'Horgan, Prince, Robbins, and Zaks, contend that if the director does not have a fresh approach to the material, then a revival becomes nothing more than an exercise. Additionally, they note that a revival should not be attempted merely for the sake of presenting the material differently; a show should be presented in a different light only if it is a better and viable interpretation of the work. (Of course, whether or not that "new" interpretation is better and viable is highly subjective.) Obviously, one must also consider the audience. Laurents points out that many regional theatres, for example, are somewhat obligated to mount re-creations in order to satisfy its audiences' tastes. This may well be true of civic, college, and high school audiences as well. Charnin makes a valid point when he states that attempting a strict re-creation of a show is an impossible task from the outset because of the incorporation of different actors who bring their own unique sensibilities and points of view to the work. Utilizing their individual talents, rather than trying to force them into cardboard cutouts of the original cast, works to the director's advantage. Other factors will also demand changes from the original. A revival of *South Pacific*, a show written to utilize a fly system and a proscenium stage, is naturally going to need adaptation if presented in-the-round, for example.

A number of directors refer to "updating" or "modernizing" a revival in an attempt to make the show more relevant for present-day audiences. This does not necessarily mean presenting the show in the current year, but rather eliminating unnecessary or questionable material or highlighting connections between the time period of the musical and the contemporary audience in attendance. In contradiction to some of the others, Charnin stresses that not every show should be "updated"; some shows simply must be presented with respect to the era in which they were created. Regarding *West Side Story* revivals he insists, "Nobody says, 'Riga tiga tum tum' [nowadays], they say, 'Fuck you, you son of a bitch.' Those people who approach it as a period piece and allow it to be directed as a period piece having reverberations to the present are the people who do successful *West Sides*."

One additional note on revivals must be made. Although it may seem an obvious conclusion, different directors create different shows. A director-choreographer will create a different version of a show than a director-writer. These directors do not create shows utilizing elements with which they are unfamiliar or uncomfortable. On the contrary, Prince says: "Where is your strong suit? My strong suit is with text. If I were a choreographer and I got into trouble, I'd probably rush right down to my feet to solve the problem. I can't do that. [I rush] to my head, to the words." Any director attempting a revival should understand the strengths and motivations the original director possessed and used to develop the work. Additionally, they should be familiar with the strengths and motivations of the book writer, lyricist, composer, designers, and actors, as well as the theatrical conventions at the time. The original artists' influence over the "finished," published script is substantial, and to ignore *how* a work developed is to limit one's depth of understanding, which may well hold the key to the revival's success. Had Prince been the driving, directorial force behind the development of *West Side Story*, for example, would the show have evolved with the strong dance element Robbins integrated into the storytelling? It seems unlikely. The more a revival director knows about the history of a show before attempting to mount it, the better equipped he or she will be to solve problems once on course toward opening night.

One additional trait these directors share is an innate adventurous spirit. At different times, and in different ways, each of the directors acknowledges an ongoing curiosity, an ever present desire to learn, a preference for the challenging over the easy. "There's this sense of wanting to learn and wanting to try it," says Daniele. "I think it's very important. If you only do what you more or less know, then you sort of get stuck." McAnuff observes, "If you have a passion for learning and for discovery, [directing's] a great thing to do." "You have to be disciplined," Prince admonishes. "You have to be educated. . . . Experience, inquisitiveness, curiosity, and a generosity of spirit. . . . All those things seem unbelievably important to me." And Wolfe explains, "I choose projects if either they scare me, or I don't know how to do them, or there's some landscape to the piece that I'm really interested in exploring . . . as opposed to something that's safe. If your fear of failure begins to define your choices, ultimately you start to suffocate your talent and your ambition and your adventurous spirit." Could this mere distinction in attitude be what separates the Broadway director from the amateur director or the local college professor? This constant inquisitiveness, curiosity, desire for exploration, and need for the challenging over the ordinary, all of which are evident in these directors, appears to be much more than mere coincidence. These traits may well be what holds the key to success in the professional American musical theatre.

Martin Charnin

Martin Charnin is the director and lyricist of one of the longest running musicals in Broadway history. *Annie* opened on April 21, 1977, and ran for 2,377 performances, surpassing long-run milestones such as *Oklahoma!* (1943), *South Pacific* (1949), and *Man of La Mancha* (1965). Charnin began his professional career in the theatre directly out of college, when he appeared on Broadway as one of the original Jets in Jerome Robbins's *West Side Story* (1957). Following that experience, and having always been interested in writing, he began to work

All quotes are taken from personal interviews conducted by the author with Mr. Charnin.

as a lyricist. "I liked the short form," he explains. "I never considered myself a novelist, and lyric writing ended up being the perfect vehicle for being able to tell a story—beginning, middle, and end—in thirty-two bars (or however long it is)." Charnin would go on to supply the lyrics for, among others, *Hot Spot* (1963) with composer Mary Rodgers, and for two shows with Mary's father Richard Rodgers: *Two By Two* (1970), and *I Remember Mama* (1979). In 1968, he turned his attention to directing, often for shows on which he also served as lyricist. His first project was *Ballad for a Firing Squad* (1968; director-lyricist), an Off-Broadway remounting of his Broadway-bound *Mata Hari* (1967; directed by Vincente Minnelli), which closed on the road. In addition to directing a number of plays, Charnin has also directed the musical revues *Nash at Nine* (1973), *Music! Music!* (1974), *Upstairs at O'Neal's* (1982; director and co-author), and *The No-Frills Revue* (1987; director and co-author), as well as the musical *Annie* (1977; director-lyricist), the London production of *Bar Mitzvah Boy* (1979), the Jackie Robinson musical *The First* (1981; director-lyricist), *Annie Warbucks* (1993; director-lyricist, a reworking of his sequel *Annie 2: Miss Hannigan's Revenge* [1990]), and the Canadian rock-opera *Jeanne La Pucelle* (1997), based on the life of Joan of Arc.

Charnin became a director because "the lyricist was the lowest man on the totem pole, and had the least power, and did the most work for the least amount of money. In the putting together of a show the director is the person who says, 'No, I'll put that song there.' 'No, let's move this actor here.' And those are the things that I thought I had the equipment and the character and the strength to do." In the midst of the concept-musical era of the '70s (Michael Bennett's *A Chorus Line*—the pinnacle of the era—had opened less than two years earlier), Charnin and his collaborators, Charles Strouse and Thomas Meehan, appeared on the scene with a "mind-bogglingly old-fashioned musical" called *Annie*. "I thought that Harold Gray [creator of the comic strip upon which the musical is based] was an American Dickens. We were coming out of a very, very angry, cynical, spiritless time. It was Vietnam, it was Nixon, it was drugs, it was awful. And Annie was the perfect manifestation of all of the promise and hope and spunk and optimism that I and my collaborators wanted not only for ourselves, [but for] our children, our country, our world." Charnin's belief that the little orphan girl could serve as a symbol of hope in a country struggling to redefine itself proved correct.

Charnin's philosophy is shaped by a single thought: "The one thing that a director cannot do in the musical theatre is *one thing*." This whole and encompassing approach dictates that "you've got to know about all of it. You cannot be uninformed. Knowledge is power. You've got to be aware of all the diverse elements; in a musical there are five times as many as in a straight play. In order to really pay that kind of attention, you can't just be single-minded and focused only on what's going up on the stage. You have to be conscious of what every department does, and what every department's idiosyncratic problem may be, so that you can prioritize; more often than not, in the crunch when you're doing a show, what you end up discovering is that everyone will have a problem and your job is to say, 'No, the costume designer's problem is, at this particular moment, more important than the orchestration.' So it's a question of having this kind of mini-quartermastering computer in your head. I think the reason wars are won is, yes, in terms of the strength of the army, but [also because] some guy makes sure that the food, and the tanks, and the guns, and the bedding, and the gasoline all get to the place where the battle is going to be fought at the same time. And so that has been an invaluable part of the process for me—knowing when to say, 'Now,' or when to say, 'Later,' or when to say, 'Never.'"

Though he does not specifically cite Jerome Robbins as being influential to his work as a director, Charnin points to *West Side Story* as having had a tremendous impact upon him. "That performance experience both helped and hurt. It helped to the extent that it showed me how a musical could have done so much of its homework beforehand that relatively few changes occurred in the eight weeks we were out of town. Jerry [Robbins] was simply engaged in detail work. No songs were cut, no songs were added. No arrangements were changed, with the possible exception of some dance stuff. No one was fired; the same company that went out came back in. Arthur [Laurents, book writer] would tinker with a line, or we would search for a way to make a crossover funnier. *West Side* is an example of a musical that was not in trouble. It *didn't* help me to the extent that it was (to my knowledge) the only musical in forty years that that ever happened to. Every show since, and probably before, has gone through a series of changes. You get rid of an actor, you change a song, a scene doesn't work, a costume is thrown out. . . . None of that happened in *West Side*. So, if that's the height of the bar at which you first experience the race, and if that's the standard by which you ultimately pursue a career, you're in deep, deep shit, because that's just never going to happen again."

Rather than learning how to direct from any one person, Charnin learned by observing the entire process. "I watched how Stephen [Sondheim] wrote lyrics. I watched how Len [Bernstein] dealt with musicians. I watched how Jerry dealt with the dancing and the stage. I watched Oliver Smith [scenic designer]. I paid attention to Irene Sharaff [costume designer]. I listened to Max Goberman [musical director]. I was just a sponge. I had my basic training in the world's most extraordinary boot camp."

Charnin's greatest influence, however, does not come from the musical theatre world, but from the dramatic world. "[Elia] Kazan has had a profound impact on me. He had a soul and he had an intellect, and a combination of the two of them. And he was a sucker for the truth. He knew how far you could push the truth, and not a lot of directors know how far you can push the truth. There were no gimmicks and tricks in the material he chose to put on the stage or in films. He also had a brilliant casting sense; and in the final analysis, many shows are made or broken by virtue of that very first choice you make as to who's going to play that part. So, he had a profound effect on me. Musical directors have had no effect upon me. I've seen their work, I've admired it, I've coveted many of the ideas they've done, but I rarely go to musicals and watch what the directors do. I go to musicals and watch what choreographers do and set designers do. To me, those two people are the necessary elements of the collaboration that I find I can't—or won't—begin a project without."

Charnin can read music "vaguely," but does not see this ability as a necessity for a director of musicals. "I think a director of musicals has to *know* music, but not necessarily to read it." Additionally, he contends a director must like the material he or she chooses to direct in order to be effective. "I think any director who simply does a job for the sake of proving that he can do the job is making a major mistake. You really have to fall in love with the material. What every one of these projects is, is a miniature love affair. It's a meeting, it's a wooing, it's a kiss, it's a courtship, it's a consummation, it's a breakup, and it's the end of a love affair. That's what they all are. I've spent a lifetime having miniature love affairs with every one of my projects. That's the kicker that sends you into the arena to begin with. If that's not there, then don't do it."

Charnin believes "directors are authors." Consequently, although he is a writer himself, he sees the director as the final editor of the script and score. "Why are directors authors? The writer will sit down and say, 'The nightclub. At a downstage table in a fully populated nightclub sit Harry and Sally.' The writer never bothered to tell anybody what the sixty other patrons in that nightclub were doing. The author is sitting there paying real strict attention to the intensity of the exchange between Harry and Sally. [The] author of the other fifty-eight people on the stage, that's me. I tell Table 1 to be drunk, and Table 2 to have a fight, and Table 3 to be asleep, and Table 4 to be dancing. . . . Nobody's writing that stuff. I'm writing it because I'm writing the directorial aspect of what I want the stage to look like while Harry and Sally are downstage in the spotlight finding out what the playwright is up to. We do that all the time. And that is writing. I don't think a writer can say he's always directing the musical, but I think a director can say he's always writing the musical." Charnin also notes that each director brings their own unique perspective to a project, which will often influence a work. "[If] a guy brings me a project, I'm going to want to change it anyway. Having nothing to do with ego, again having only to do with point of view." Because of that, he prefers to involve himself with a project in the very earliest stages. This allows his point of view to be incorporated from the outset and results in fewer changes during the process.

He looks upon a work as never being "finished" or "complete." Consequently, he states, "I've always gone into rehearsals without a complete libretto and score. Because they're never finished. And even when they get finished and they're up, they're not finished. That's part of the fun of it. They keep on changing." This willingness to allow a work to evolve continuously throughout the process ultimately produces the best interpretation of the show at any given time. Although he has directed a number of other people's works, he prefers to direct shows for which he is also one of the writers. Acting as a writer benefits him as a director by giving him multiple perspectives on the material: writing it, re-creating it as a director during pre-production, and then mounting the amalgamation of the two on stage with the actors.

Charnin directs plays differently than he does musicals. "You have to approach a play differently. A musical is two hours, and an hour of it is singing and dancing. A play is two hours, and it's two hours of talking and staging and behavior." In a musical, "when you're in trouble you can always say, 'Well, let's start the vamp here.'" Though his approach to the two forms is different (and he does not see one as more difficult to mount than the other), he recognizes that plays and musicals have inherent similarities that need to be acknowledged. "I think they all have rhythm. I think they all have a dynamic. I think they all have a tempo. I think they all have music. Sometimes the music is notes, and sometimes it's just language." This is exemplified in Charnin's approach to *Cafe Crown*, an Off-Broadway play he directed at the Joseph Papp Public Theatre: "It's a play about the Yiddish theatre. It needed the 'music' of that time, and the dialect and the jargon and the rhythms of the language of those people who were hanging around on Second Avenue in 1942. And that's music. And that music had to just simply be there, because lines would not get laughs, and beats would not be understood unless that music were played accurately." Recognizing the inherent music and rhythm of a piece, regardless of its genre, is vitally important.

He believes most directors, including himself, need to be somewhat dictatorial in order to mount a production: "We all have to be benevolent despots. There's no way to get a show on [otherwise]." He recognizes that during the course of his career he has become both more and less "tyrannical." "More to the extent that as you gain knowledge you kind of know what will work and what won't work. Less to the extent that you realize that you don't know everything. So, the things that you do know, that do work, you kind of have to hold hard and fast to; and the things that you [don't know, that's when you have to] allow the concept of collaboration to make the material happen." By acquiring a knowledge of the entire production a director can better delegate responsibility to those people who can solve potential problems as, or before, they arise. Thus, though forceful in "steering this armada across an ocean to the shore," Charnin is quite open to the input of his collaborators with whom he surrounds himself. "You have to have the biggest ego on the block and not display it. You listen to everybody, but you have to filter it. Somebody may say something absolutely splendid and bright, and you have to be big enough to accept it, and not feel threatened because they found it and you didn't. It's not going to say in the program 'Exit in the second scene by Joe Blow' if it says directed by you!" This openness to other's ideas was reinforced after Charnin suffered a heart attack in 1980. "It elevated the level of the quality of people I collaborated with because I gave them more responsibility. And therefore, my heart attack made them do a lot more work, and better work I think." Because of the personal and professional trust that builds up over time, he prefers to work with the same collaborators from show to show when possible. This allows for a development and use of a shorthand communication between collaborators, which can ultimately make for a faster, more efficient work environment. This is critically important as he places far more significance on working quickly nowadays than he did earlier in his career. "It's vitally important to get work done fast. There isn't the luxury of time. Time has become an enemy because time suddenly became money. And when money and time meet, the artist gets creamed."

When approaching revivals, Charnin believes recognizing the era in which the show was written should have a great influence over how the production is remounted, if it is revived at all. "Take *Hair* [1968; directed on Broadway by Tom O'Horgan], for example. Done in the '60s. It couldn't have been in the '50s. And it could not be done in the same way, with its truth, unless it was done in its own time. That's why revivals of *Hair* don't make any sense. Similarly, revivals of *West Side* don't make any sense. Because they try to make *West Side* a contemporary piece. It's not a contemporary piece, it's a period piece. It has to be done as it was. I mean, nobody says, 'Riga tiga tum tum' [nowadays], they say, 'Fuck you, you son of a bitch.' If you don't approach it as a 'then'—if you approach it as a 'now'—you are really in trouble." At the same time, he believes that re-creating a duplicate of the original production is an almost impossible goal because of the new and different personalities of those artists working on the new production. His 1997 Broadway revival of *Annie*, for example, changed considerably from the original, "because [different] actors do it differently. The vulnerability in one actor was not there; the way two people bump into one another was not the same; the way a cop looks at a kid was not there in the same way. It all changes." He believes that that particular production suffered due to confusion over whether it was to be done as a new production, or to be re-created as the 1977 experience. "I kept screaming, 'You can't duplicate it.' Because there is no other Dorothy Loudon, there is no other Andrea McArdle, there is no other Reid Shelton—they're all going to be different!"

Charnin does "preparation of every kind known to man" during pre-production. "A good director, I believe, is never surprised. There are no surprises when you finally hit the stage. There are no surprises in the casting because you've been there. You've gone into endless pre-production work with your scenic designer so that you know how the transitions are made; you know how sets come on, how they go off, you know what they're going to look like. You've seen sketches from the costume designer, and you've seen color swatches so you know the palette of the costume design matches the palette of what the set is going to look like. You talk about how you're going to light the show with the lighting designer." Obtaining a sense of the entire physical production (sets, costumes, lights) is one of the most important tasks for the director during pre-production, and Charnin finds his education in art (he holds a B.F.A. in painting) serves him well in this regard. "Just the ability to understand things visually: colors, textures, sizes, shapes, whatnot." The director should have an answer for every question; yet at the same time the director should recognize that aspects of the show will undoubtedly change during the course of its development, thus possibly forcing future answers to be different. Though he strives for a comprehensive understanding of the show prior to rehearsals, he admits, "You can only do so much pre-production on paper before you actually get bodies up on the stage, [because] the space changes, and that which you thought was going to happen between two paper actors changes. Because they all bring their own individual characteristics to the event."

For Charnin, casting is "the great turning point in a show." He likes to have people read from the script as much as possible at auditions. "In musicals you kind of know after thirty-two bars [of their audition song] whether or not they can hit the notes and whether or not they have rhythm. The big question is whether or not they can *act*; unless you're doing a really sung-through kind of musical where there is not that much nonmusical material being done," when a less-accomplished actor will sometimes suffice. He prefers seeing different combinations of actors together to find out "how they bounce off of one another. I like to bring groups of actors in and have them read. If it's a scene with three people, I'll have readings with three people at a time as opposed to having a stage manager do the other part of the reading. It kind of gives you infor-mation which amplifies your instincts." This also helps him cast a com-pany with similar acting styles, which he deems important for bringing about a consistent and cohesive work. Unfortunately, he notes, a direc-tor never has the luxury of being able to have the entire ensemble of actors in the audition room at the same time to find out how they are going to respond chemically to one another. But Charnin attempts to comprise a company he believes is compatible through these mini-groupings. Because he is a lyricist as well as a director, it is not surpris-ing that he also puts emphasis on the performer who can act through a song. "You're acting when you're *saying* words, there's no question about it." But, in a musical, "you have to understand that more than the notes are what are carrying the song. They've got to understand a *lyric*."

He has gained a great deal of experience auditioning children from his numerous productions of *Annie* and *Annie Warbucks*. "I've found that with children in particular, they're really like an empty drawing tablet. I mean, if they're super highly trained and focused at the age of nine I'd be very surprised. The ones who swallow their name when they say it are kids that you know you're not going to be able to get a performance out of. But the ones that stand in front of you and fold their arms and say, 'My name is Samantha and I'm ten!' really give you a sense of confidence. Part of casting children is my own instinct about trusting that they're going to work out, because I have to believe that a kid is really going to deliver." His approach to auditioning children differs from his approach to casting adults. Recognizing that, with the exception of Annie herself, the orphan girls in *Annie* "are not multidimensional characters" due simply to their lack of stage time, Charnin places the emphasis in casting more on personality than trained acting ability: "They have to have energy, and a good attention span, and good strong voices, and be able to keep in formation, and they have to be able to look you in the eye and not be timid or shy about being on stage." Additionally, he judges them on how they conduct themselves during the course of the audition. He does not have the orphan girls read from the script. Instead, "if they cut the mustard as singers and dancers," he chooses to interact with them personally through short improvisations. Once he has chosen the orphan girls he casts them without making specific character determinations. "They're assigned as 'orphans' as opposed to individual characters with the one exception of the character of Molly who is the baby; that has to be a size determination." This allows him time during the course of the rehearsal process to better judge their personalities, abilities, and how they interact with the other children before settling on specific characters for each. When auditioning girls for the role of Annie, "we take a lot more time because the burden is a lot greater. She's what the show's about."

In this case he reads and sings the girls much like he does the adults he auditions.

The secret to working with children, according to Charnin, is to not treat them like children. "I'm not saying not to *know* that they're children. But not to coddle them. Treat them as actors. My relationship to the kids is really interesting. I'm half terror, and half Pied Piper, which is exactly what I want to be. They're scared to death of me, but by the same token, if I say, 'Come on, let's all leap into the river!' they'll all run right after me and swim!" He believes this aspect of "terror" present between himself and the child actors is necessary. It is what keeps them from losing focus and insures the professional integrity of the process and the production. "They have to know how far they can go with me. There is a terrible, terrible discipline problem with some kids, which not only affects that individual kid and the kid [she] is working with, but the grown-up actors who have not got the kind of patience quotient for children. Some of them don't have children. Some of them don't *like* children." Therefore, Charnin incorporates an approach of disciplined play when working with child actors.

Though his shows have often been led by big-name stars, Charnin contends, "The most important thing in a show is the show. I like stars, I work with stars, I've had success with stars, I've had failures with stars. But to me it's the event." He believes stars enhance a project, but just as he does not coddle his child actors, neither does he coddle his stars. He finds that some big-name performers, though benefiting the production, can sometimes be detrimental to the process almost entirely because of the actor's insecurity. "There have been stars who are so scared [they] have to be attended to, not only on stage, but offstage. And they drain you, because you just have so much in you to be able to deal with an entire company. If the star is taking up all your time, you have very little left."

He begins the rehearsal process with an initial read-through. He finds

this very helpful for gaining a sense of how much the company understands the material, whether it is an original work or a revival. "When
you're doing a brand-new play, obviously, you've never heard it before—
really never heard it before." This read-through then helps flesh out the
characters and the story, which up to that point may only have been
heard in the director's head. "When you're doing a revival, when you're
doing a re-creation, you have a sense of what the material should sound
like. You know where the stresses are, you know where the accents are,
you know where the jokes are, you know where the tears are. So, one
of the things that I do is sit there and listen to see just what the actors'
instincts are in relationship to the material." This gives him a better
sense of how much script analysis will be needed later in the rehearsal
process. Following that, he spends at least a week with the cast learning the music. "I teach a score before I teach a script." He does not
entirely set the script aside: "On occasion you go back once or twice
during the course of that first week and you remind them what the play's
about. But I tell them not to memorize anything, with the exception of
the musical material," which very rarely changes. Charnin dedicates the
second week of rehearsals to reading and analyzing the script. "I don't
like to get shows up on their feet [right away]. I don't like to block until
people have a real sense of what the play's about. I try to keep that going
at the table in the chairs for as long as possible, within the confines of
the reality of how much time you have to mount the project. You can't
be that indulgent where you just sit around the table until the week
before you go into the theatre." He is quick to point out, however, that
shows often change once they get up on their feet and that too much
analyzing can be self-defeating. "It's like a piece of cheese in the refrig-
erator: you just know it's going to go bad tomorrow, so you'd better eat
it tonight." Only after the cast has a solid understanding of the characters and the story (generally after about a week of study around the
table) does he commence with blocking the show.

"I block it in my head. I don't do paper blocking. I've found that to be pointless. I have to really acquaint myself with the physical production. I have to know how the scenery comes in which makes a determination as to whether or not some event can occur stage left or stage right, and where the furniture is going to be, and whether or not an actor has enough time to make a costume change. It's very technical to the extent that the actor probably feels abandoned." Charnin does not necessarily encourage input from his actors when blocking, but is often open to suggestions if they are made. "I mean, if he says, 'Why doesn't he *limp* over there?' and it makes perfect sense . . . you take advantage of these moments. They're all 'found' moments, and there are many found moments in a play. And part of the fun of it is finding them. Otherwise, it's a singularly boring process if all you're doing is saying, 'Go there, go there, go there, go there.' You have to keep an open mind when you're doing a show. You may have had an idea in your head that it could only be done this way because it's the only way you've ever heard it, and then some very clever actor comes in and gives you an entirely different take. It can be something very external like saying, 'I think I'll play this character with a cold,' or it can be something very internal which says 'this character has a deep resentment toward his father and that colors every word that I say.' When that [discovery] occurs, you're a fool if you don't take advantage of the collaborative process. A director has to be as much a sponge to an actor's ideas as an actor has to be a sponge to a director's and a writer's ideas."

Throughout the rehearsal process Charnin prefers to have the entire cast in attendance, especially with a new musical, because changes often occur without warning. "I may change my mind . . . and decide I want to take a look at this scene because I just got an idea." Having the company on hand should he want to instantaneously change the schedule allows for the spontaneity of creativity to be immediately acted upon. In addition, rather than give actors notes individually, "I think it's important that notes be given collectively, because I think that everybody learns about the play, and my approach to the play, if they're all sitting there hearing the notes at the same time." This goes for big stars as well as the chorus. Having everyone in attendance receiving notes together eliminates unexpected "surprises," such as a "new line reading, a new beat, a new attitude, a new piece of behavior" that might be jarring for another performer on stage who was not aware of the change ahead of time.

Technical rehearsals, Charnin thinks, can be a time when the actors may feel directorless. He regards this as a problem inherent to the process: "[During technical rehearsals] we're walking through the scene but I'm paying more attention to whether or not the lights are in the right place, or whether the costume fits." To avoid actors' uneasiness, he prepares them ahead of time. "I kind of make a speech to them all the time that, 'there are going to be five or ten times in the course of this process that you will feel that you are simply *abandoned*,' and I use that word specifically because that's basically what's happening." Ideally, this allows the actors to continue the growth and development of their characters individually while other, more technical areas of the production take the spotlight. Once the show moves into previews, Charnin is able to refocus his attention on the actors. With the aid of an audience's reaction to the show, he can then begin solving problems that may become evident only in a performance situation. He recalls the previews of *Annie*: "We were a week old at Goodspeed [Opera House in Connecticut] back in 1976 when it became apparent that the young lady who was playing the part [of Annie] just didn't have the grit and the spunk and the streetwise quality which really gave us the right take on the role, and we had to let her go." The difference was "I got the opportunity to have her up in front of an audience and I saw the response." In the midst of previews, spunky Andrea McArdle took over the role.

After opening, Charnin admits, "I don't like to go back, but I do." He suggests that time away from a production can often give a director a fresh perspective on the work and allow for obvious corrections that may have been overlooked during the technical process of mounting a show. When not in attendance personally he depends upon the stage manager and dance captain to act as his surrogates, both of whom are authorized to give notes on his behalf. This, he believes, saves time in rectifying problems: "If I've hired a good stage manager, the assumption is that he's going to correct it on the spot, as opposed to going through the process of tracking me down to ask me these questions. He'll make these adjustments." Regarding cast replacements he notes, "[The show] always comes to life yet again when a new actor comes into the role." For that reason he will at times rehearse new cast replacements himself. However, since he believes a qualified stage manager can often do the job as well as the director, he will just as often turn over the job of rehearsing a replacement to them.

"I think if you asked any Broadway writer, or director, or choreographer, they would say that they would give their eyeteeth to be able to say, 'We open in Boston, play six weeks, and then come to New York.' Hardly anybody does that anymore. Out-of-town tryouts have become a thing of the past." The alternative "is to go and do these endless, relentless workshops." Workshops, taken individually, cost less and provide a controlled audience from which to gather opinions, recommendations, and criticisms. But one workshop can merely lead to a second, and a second to a third. Charnin points out the irony: "If you do it five times you're actually, in point of fact, equaling the cost of what one out-of-town venture [costs]." Earlier in his career, "we used to go through the workshop process by doing backer's auditions in order to raise money. If you pay attention during the course of the backer's audition you glean a great deal from the hundred and fifty people." What is lost by the elimination of out-of-town tryouts, he contends, is the freedom to fail without losing the project altogether. "When I say failing I don't mean crumbling in front of your eyes, but defining a problem, agonizing over how to solve it, [and] solving it. That sense of everybody being in the boat together, the communal feeling of everybody working toward making something better and a hit, is really gone."

He views the regional theatre system as having taken up some of the slack in preparing shows for Broadway and has often utilized it in honing his own shows. "That's one of the reasons I like places like Goodspeed. I really think it's a valuable proving ground mostly from a creative person's standpoint to the extent that you're in the middle of nowhere (hopefully), not under the supercritical eyes of your colleagues and the New York press. You can fail in a regional theatre and still continue to work. You can't fail on Broadway and continue to work." However, in the years since he mounted the original production of *Annie* at Goodspeed in 1976, he believes that regional theatres have "grown up," and their attitude and approach to new works has changed. "[Years ago] the regional theatre system had a different set of ground rules [and] they were sort of satisfied with being the proving ground for new material. [Nowadays] they're not willing to excuse as easily the concept of a 'work in progress,' and therefore the skill you have to have approaching the first draft is almost equal to the skill you have to have—but less of the knowledge—of the third draft. Because you learn things. And we're not allowed to learn things in the regional theatres anymore."

He believes the university system could be influential in the development of new works, but thinks its primary focus is often elsewhere: "What they're really developing are performers." According to Charnin, since acting programs often receive top priority, directing programs appear "tacked on" and are therefore ineffective: "[The] reason is that there aren't any highly qualified people who were in the trenches teaching how it works. And directing is not something you can do on paper.

It's like fighting paper wars: not a lot is at risk when all you're drawing are Xs and Os on a piece of paper." He believes the best way to learn to direct the musical is through "on-the-job training. If you get a job in the regional theatre system, you're at least in the trenches. And you're watching other directors work, and learning. And maybe not learning what to do, but perhaps learning what *not* to do. And that's basically where the directors are coming from. They're not necessarily coming from the colleges or the universities."

As far as producers go, he believes the "era of producers" ended in 1991 with the death of Joseph Papp. "He was the last of the producers. Before Joe there were the Kermit Bloomgardens of this world, and the David Merricks of this world, and the Bobby Fryers of this world, and these guys were producers. They didn't intrude, they let you go as far as they believed you should go. They paid attention. They were there. They spent their money. They were really wise. They were not accountants. They were not misguided businessmen." The lack of such top-notch producers in the theatre ultimately makes a director's job in mounting a show nowadays more difficult. "The money people . . . [are] doing things like focus groups and auditioning material for people who are giving them feedback, and it's become a situation where a lot of musicals are being made by committee. And maybe one works, but in the long run what it does is it robotizes the process."

In addition to book musicals, Charnin has directed a number of musical revues. For revues he adopts a different directing focus. "Your programming is entirely different. You're dealing with an anthology of short stories. You have to populate the pages in a totally different way. There are two different kinds of musical revues: there are revues like *Upstairs at O'Neal's,* which had no basic, unifying theme—and then there's *Diamonds* in which everything had something to do with baseball." That distinction will often dictate how the "programming" of the show is arranged, although Charnin sees some common rules that apply to both. "You're not going to put three ballads next to one another, you're not going to put two duets next to one another. Revues invariably are more prone to structural changes than shows are. You discover that you can lift a whole piece, or three pieces, and throw them into the second act. But you can't necessarily monkey around with a plot and decide, 'Let's burn Joan of Arc in the second *scene!*'" His years of experience with revues have influenced his work with musicals. "I think it viscerally informs how I will do it. I think musical theatre, when things are exotic and full of surprises, is the most interesting kind of theatre that exists. [But] when you keep on relentlessly hitting people over the head with the same kind of event, the same kind of musical number that has yet another key change eight bars after the last, after a while the audience says, 'Okay, give me a break.' So, I bring that revue mentality to the [musical]. You wouldn't, for example, do nine kid numbers in a row in *Annie*. After a while the audience would say, 'My God, get me out of here!' But programming usually has a lot to do with how skillfully you can create moments on the stage that can take the audience to a place that they have no expectation of going," whether in a revue or a musical. "It's like getting on a roller coaster. They get on it, and they're scared to death, but they know they're strapped in; and they'll scream and yell and have a terrific time on the ride. When you don't feel like you're strapped in, you're in trouble."

Charnin is also one of the few directors to attempt a musical sequel, a practice with few successes. Sequels such as *Bring Back Birdie* (1981) and *The Best Little Whorehouse Goes Public* (1994) were given little attention. To date, only James Lapine's *Falsettoland* (1990) has found an audience. Charnin approached *Annie 2: Miss Hannigan's Revenge* in a different manner than his other musicals: "You approach it differently because you have all of this baggage . . . [which] you have to do two things with. One, I have to believe going in that everybody saw *Annie* in order for me to start an *Annie 2*. (That's when an assumption becomes a presumption.) I couldn't do that. Therefore, I lost a considerable amount of time laying the ground rules to remind the audience in the first part of *Annie 2* what the hell *Annie 1* was all about. Then [two,] you have the responsibility of making it entertaining in its own right." Eventually, the goal proved unattainable, and the show closed in Washington, D.C., before ever making its way to Broadway. Charnin, however, refused to let the material go to waste. He continued a "constant reduction process" that entailed reworking the book and rearranging the score. He eventually opened Off Broadway six years later with a new sequel, *Annie Warbucks*. "I knew I had made a mistake in Washington and I had to redeem myself, and any venue that allowed me redemption was perfectly acceptable."

By keeping his sights fixed firmly on the production as a whole Charnin avoids being sidetracked with unnecessary goals that may throw a show out of balance. "I believe that when I do a show, I'm doing a show. I'm not doing my show, I'm not doing the composer's show, I'm not doing the book writer's show, I'm not doing the producer's show, I'm not doing the star's show—I'm doing the show's show. And the show's show is all of those elements." Ultimately, the director's job is not something to be held onto, but a gift one gives to others: "I'm very fat and pregnant at the beginning of a show. By the time opening night comes, I have passed everything in me over to somebody else. They have then taken it and done what they're going to do with it. I'm empty at the end of a show, absolutely empty. I'm running on fumes. At that point, they own it. Also in this process I'm saying to them, 'You can do it better than I can do it.' I've got to make them believe that. So, by the end, if I do my job well, they do believe it. And if I do my job really well, they believe it and forget that I had anything to do with it. There are three ways to do anything in a musical: the right way, the wrong way, and my way. And sometimes, hopefully, my way and the right way are one and the same."

Graciela Daniele

Graciela Daniele made her Broadway debut as a dancer in *What Makes Sammy Run?* (1964) before assisting choreographer Michael Bennett on a number of musicals, including *Coco* (1969), *Follies* (1971), and *Seesaw* (1973). With the encouragement of Bennett and director-choreographer Bob Fosse with whom she also worked, Daniele began choreographing in the mid-'70s, eventually staging, among others, Wilford Leach's acclaimed revival of *The Pirates of Penzance* (1981), *The Rink* (1984), *The Mystery of Edwin Drood* (1985), *The Goodbye Girl*

All quotes are taken from personal interviews conducted by the author with Ms. Daniele.

(1993), and *Ragtime* (1998). In 1986, Max Ferra, the head of INTAR (a New York theatre dedicated to Hispanic artists) said to her, "Grazie, you should develop something *you* want. What do *you* want to do?" That invitation led to her first project as director-choreographer, *Tango Apasionado* (1987). She took on the directing reins by default: "It was because I created something that I *had* to direct because nobody understood what I wanted to do except me." Since that time she has directed and choreographed *Once on This Island* (1990), a Broadway revival of *Annie Get Your Gun* (1999; co-choreographed by Jeff Calhoun), and while serving as resident director at Lincoln Center Theatre, *Hello Again* (1994), *Chronicle of a Death Foretold* (1995), *A New Brain* (1998), and *Marie Christine* (1999).

Born in Argentina, Daniele was enrolled in the Teatro Colon in Buenos Aires at age seven at the suggestion of a doctor who believed the strenuous ballet work would help correct a malformation in the arch of her feet. The suggestion led to a career. She eventually moved to Paris where she continued to study and perform the ballet's traditional repertory but found herself unfulfilled: "There was not enough plot, there was not enough acting." Then fate intervened when she attended a performance of the European touring production of *West Side Story* (1957). "I realized, 'Oh my God, this is what I want to do! I want to be able to tell a story through dance. I want to be like these people.' But I didn't know the language—the jazz language. So, I came to New York to study." Within a month she had landed a role dancing on Broadway. Working as a choreographer, let alone a director, was far from a goal early in her career, but as she began to assist Bennett in his work, she realized she was much more interested in "using the creative mind, as opposed to using just the performing side. Bennett and Fosse . . . were very encouraging. They thought that I had the creativity for it, so they not only inspired me, but they sort of pushed me towards trying it. You always have to have that person who says, 'You can do it!'"

Bennett and Fosse (and Jerome Robbins indirectly with *West Side Story*) were extremely influential in her development as a director in the musical theatre. While assisting Bennett, for example, she says, "I had the opportunity and the luck of being in the same room while decisions were being made. I was present in the wonderful creative process. This is where you really learn, when you see somebody else who's brilliant at work." Although she contends she does not direct a musical in the same way Bennett did, she notes that by observing him she learned ways of solving problems. Specifically, she learned what questions to ask: "What is the intention of the moment? What is this scene about? How can I transform this moment into something else? All of these things, coming from the world of ballet as I did, were totally new to me." With this intense education in the professional theatre, it is not surprising that she favors an apprenticeship approach for student-directors to learn how to direct the musical. "I always say to my assistants and associates, 'When there is a problem, I will solve it, but solve it in your mind before I even talk.' That's how you learn. Then the master goes and does it, of course, but then you compare. You go, 'Ahh, I see why he or she did that. If I had done it . . . ' It's all about keeping your eyes very open, and your ears very open, and your mouth shut until they ask you something."

She does not believe that the student-director makes these personal discoveries through university training programs, but rather through experience that can only come from working within the process. "It's not academic at all. I mean, you can go that way, but I don't think that is the real process. Many directors come from the academic world: they go off to college, they specialize in theatre, and all that. But you have to remember that I come from the dance world where the academic is really physical work. Academic background might help you, might make it easy, might actually get you more jobs faster. [But] I think it's just the doing. To me, the verb 'to know' is not to be informed; the verb 'to know' something means to experience how to solve the problem. So, academic background might be very good, [but] I didn't have any and it didn't stop me. In my case, it was experience and luck. And being awake for the opportunit[ies] instead of letting them pass me by."

Integrated dance within the structure of the musical has always been her greatest aspiration and what eventually led her to directing. "The directing part actually came from a certain amount of frustration of the dance on Broadway; it was somewhat limited. There was something in me that was saying, 'I wish I could do more than what I do. I wish I could test myself more. I wish I could experiment more in the musical theatre.' Not thinking about directing still. I was thinking about how to be able to do more in my own field [choreography]." When Max Ferra's offer came to develop a project at INTAR, it seemed the natural next step for her.

Her goal when developing a piece is "not to go with the formula of the American musical, but to try to introduce dance more as a very creative force. Not just as entertainment, but as an integral part of telling the story. To take all the forms and throw them out the window and start from scratch, as I attempted with *Chronicle* [*of a Death Foretold*]. You can't do *Oklahoma!* [1943] again. That would be a step backwards." She also directs in a way that allows dance to come from anywhere in the story: "Dance doesn't have to be steps. Dance is walking with an intention on a certain beat. Dance is standing up and sitting down. Dance is making love. Dance is having a child. Dance is fighting. If you stylize it to music, it's dance."

What does not interest her, however, is dance merely for the sake of entertainment. "I never enjoyed, in the musical theatre, the 'dance break.' Sixteen bars, or thirty-two bars of a bunch of merry villagers kicking their legs! I always had to understand *why* people danced. Because 'dance break' to me means entertainment. I came to this country because of *West Side Story*. There was not one second of fluffiness or 'entertainment' there. Everything that happened on that stage was extremely dramatic, or very funny. But it was all about characters, plot, and intentions." Although she came up through the ranks as a dancer and then a choreographer, she does not feel that her shows have a greater focus on dance than other directors. "I don't think I'm one of the most 'dancing' directors around. I am in the theatre because I like storytelling. And if the story's told through a song, or it's told through a scene, or it's told through movement, to me it's still telling the story."

Women directors or director-choreographers are not new to the American musical theatre (Agnes de Mille served as director-choreographer on two Broadway productions midway through her career: Rodgers and Hammersteins's *Allegro* [1947] and Cole Porter's *Out of This World* [1950]), but they have been few and far between throughout the latter half of the century. Daniele has never had a problem finding employment as a director in the nonprofit/regional theatres and believes most women directors find the same openness in that forum. She contends, however, that the commercial theatre is different; there directing is "a male-dominated field." The reason for this, according to Daniele, is because a producer ("even if it is a woman") is always going to look to hire the "most renowned and experienced directors" when bringing a new show to Broadway; "there's no time or money to fool around with new people . . . because you've got one chance." Because the commercial theatre has been a male-oriented field for so long, a majority of renowned and experienced directors are men. Therefore, more men than women have the credentials that producers seek, and consequently men continue to obtain a majority of the directing positions. This pattern obviously limits opportunities for women—the one thing they need most in order to compete with their male counterparts.

"Because it has been like that for such a long time it's going to take a while before it changes. But it will change, because there are too many extraordinary women directors out there: Julie Taymor, Susan Schulman. . . . The only reason why I am doing it is because I have the chutzpah." Daniele suggests that producers' perceptions are slowly beginning to change and points to Julie Taymor's appointment as director of Disney's stage adaptation of *The Lion King* as an example. Because of Taymor's unique style, Daniele says, "they went and hired the 'artist'—it just happens that it was a woman." Ultimately, although she would like to see more women directing in the commercial musical theatre, she holds no animosity toward her male counterparts. Indeed her greatest influences, support, and inspiration have come from men. If they are the path into the musical theatre, then women should embrace rather than shun them, she believes.

Daniele prefers working as both director and choreographer on her shows. This generally means more work for her, but in the long run it makes her job easier: "Because of the simple reason that it doesn't matter how close you are to the director or your collaborators, you are not inside of their minds." Wearing both hats simultaneously brings about a more consistent and singular vision to the work, although she knows some shows require more diversification: "*Ragtime* [for which she served as choreographer under Frank Galati's direction] is so huge, I don't know if one person could have done it." She sees the heyday of the director-choreographer (the likes of Robbins, Kidd, Fosse, Bennett, and Champion) as a passing era. However, her firmly established roots in the dance world are never abandoned. "I am a director-choreographer. I can't ever forget the choreographic. Even when I do a straight play. I don't mean that by dancing—doing steps—but the idea of the structure of something, of working with music, or dealing even with the text as music, and thinking in those terms. That's my world so I can never deny it."

When choosing her projects, Daniele seeks out weighty material. She attributes this to her education in the Teatro Colon, which demanded not only participation in a great many of the Teatro's ballets and operas but also the attendance of them. "I remember being transported by this incredible music and these incredible *stories*. That, I think, influenced me to search for something that is a little deeper than just light entertainment in the musical theatre; [for] something that moves you somehow, either by laughter or by tears. I like contemporary Greek theatre. Death, and sex, and jealousy! That's juicy." She prefers projects she can "get passionately involved with, or [which are] extremely challenging." She does not necessarily have to like the material, as long as "it feels like it's going to make me grow, and go deeper than I have up to now." Ironically, this passion for the work is not a requirement for her when merely serving as choreographer. "As a choreographer I can get away with it. Because it's a little more separate. As a choreographer, you can be as a designer—a little more clinical, and just bring your craft into it. But as a director you have to be so passionate about what you're doing. Because it's not only about craft. You have to inspire a lot of people."

She develops each of her original musicals through three progressive periods: the "talking" period, the "pregnancy" period, and finally the rehearsal period. "The first is the talking period. Just talk, talk, talk. You must not be afraid or shy about just vomiting everything out, even if it's stupid. [This creates] a sense of freedom in everybody. You can say the most outrageous thing in the world, and nobody's going to put you down. Because that outrageous thing might not be right, but it might *trigger* a great idea. The second period is the time where I go with just the skeletonical part of the score and my assistant into a room alone. And think and walk and move and talk and let all this process start giving me the pregnancy." The primary focus during this "pregnancy" period is on "putting all the elements together. What do I want to say in this moment? What is the song about? What is the intention of this song? What does it say about the character? If we are dancing, why are we dancing? What is it that propels us? All the directorial questions of those particular songs. And the third one is, of course, the rehearsal period when you get the actors. And you have to communicate all of this that you have learned in a way that they think *they* are finding it out—as opposed to you telling them. Because that's the best way of directing: looking like you're not directing."

Daniele believes the primary objective for a director during pre-production is "to immerse one's self in the musical or play" and thereby obtain a complete intellectual and emotional understanding of it. Without a firm grasp on the show prior to rehearsals, a director cannot hope to guide a company of actors to find it for themselves. Daniele does this by conducting research into the period of the piece, going to museums and viewing art of the period to develop a sense of culture, style, and time, and by bringing her own life experience to the work to create a fully dimensional understanding of the world of the play. This she learned from her mentors. "One thing that both [Bennett and Fosse] did—and most of the great [directors] that I've worked with have done—was an enormous amount of research and an enormous amount of pre-production." This is not only done for new works, but for revivals as well. "*Annie Get Your Gun* is a revival, but to me, because I've never seen it, it's a new show." When approaching the revival of *Annie Get Your Gun*, her goal was to make "a contemporary piece out of it, [while] at the same time being very respectful of the period and the magic of the score and the book." Here she is not referring to updating the work (although the book was revised by Peter Stone), but to bringing her personal sensibility to the work: "How do I see it—a woman stepping into the twenty-first century—how do I see a 1940s musical?"

In addition to research, Daniele works diligently to establish "a very close relationship with the authors, because they are the ones who did it; they are the ones who wrote it down. So, I want to fish out of them, not how they see it or how it should look, because that's not what's important, but what it means to them. So that I can really understand and sort of digest it and translate it to the actors. I am an interpreter of their dreams. Without them we wouldn't be there." Though her goal is to interpret the writers' work, she admits that it is the director, and not the authors, who must serve as the final editor of the script and score. "There has to be a captain, especially in musicals. There are so many people involved, and there are so many people with opinions, and wonderful opinions, and one should listen to everybody as a director. But there's got to be, eventually, one person who makes the final decision. I'll give you an example: in *Once on This Island* our favorite song was an eleven o'clock [number] called 'When Daniel Marries Me.' It was one of the most beautiful, lyrical pieces I have ever heard. We all loved it. [But when] we did the workshop . . . every time we got to that point you could feel the uneasiness in the house. So, I finally had to face Lynn [Ahrens, librettist] and Steven [Flaherty, composer] and say, 'This song is not working.' So, out went the best song." In Daniele's process, after first serving as editor, she then becomes a collaborator. "I didn't say to them, 'Write another song.' The only thing that I said was, 'She [the character] has to be absolutely free, and it has to be a triumphant moment for her.' And so they created a little dance [in which] she just throws the shoes away and she *dances*." The beloved "When Daniel Marries Me" was ultimately replaced by the more appropriate "Ti Moune's Dance," and the uneasiness in the audience was replaced with joy.

Daniele's final editorial decision-making power also extends to design elements, yet she is careful to allow her designers to find their own truth in the piece and bring their own talents to interpreting the work. "I don't tell them what to do. I give them the piece to read and then we have meetings, and I listen to what they feel—their instant emotional reaction to it. Then we talk in general terms. And then I talk about what I think the piece is about, and what the author thinks. (I involve the author, sometimes, in those preliminary talks.) [But] this is not about designing, this is not about saying, 'This is what we're going to do.' It is just talking." Daniele prefers this to making any immediate, crippling decisions early in the process. Believing designers not only *can* be, but also *should* be influential on the overall work, she likes to have her team of designers on board from the very beginning of a project (the "talking" period) so that the design elements can evolve and develop as the script does.

"I always felt that the good directors I worked with were very good at casting and surrounding themselves with the right people as designers and collaborators. If you can get that, fifty percent of the battle is won." Although she notes the importance of casting, she is not an advocate of the process. "I hate auditions. When I was a dancer I hated them, when I became a choreographer I hated them, and now as a director I hate them. I think it is just so sad that there is no other way of doing it. You have to put those poor actors through such a sense of expectation, and a sense of rejection. It's horrible." She tries to counter this by making her auditions as "fun and light" as possible and will often get up and shake each auditioner's hand to bring a human touch to the process. "I think it's terribly difficult for them and for me: for them to be what they can be and who they are, and for me to see it in five or ten minutes. I usually tell my actors, 'Don't forget that when you walk into that room, even if there are twenty people behind the table, those twenty people want you to be the one! We don't hate you. On the contrary, we are praying that you are going to be so perfect that you're going to get the job.'" While she bases a good deal of the weight of the audition on talent (appropriate to the needs of the character on the page), she also relies on instinct when casting, a lesson she learned from friend and director Wilford Leach. "It's like dogs smell. Look at two dogs. They look at each other, they smell each other, and either their hair goes up in the back and they start growling, or they start romping around like puppies and they want to play. I think that's what it is. It's not only the talent of the actor, but do I want to play with them for the next three months? Do I want to be ten to twelve hours a day in the same room playing with them? It's an instinct." Additionally, she looks for actors who are direct and honest. "Now, it's so hard, because how direct and honest can you be in ten minutes when your legs are shaking and you want a job? But there is a certain quality that actors have. They come in and they say, 'This is me. Like me or not, but this is me.'" When this quality is accompanied by talent, and her instinct about an actor is positive, then Daniele has confidence in her casting choices.

Although a dancer and choreographer herself, she does not cast only dancer-actors and will at times cast performers with little dancing ability if she believes they are right for the role. "I adore actors, and I have sometimes hired actors that could not move at all because I know I'm going to make them move! Once I get through with them they're going to feel free physically. Because dance is not only about steps; it's not about technique. In the dance world, that's what it is. In the theatre world, it's the ability of being comfortable with your body—being a physical actor. So, the moment they free themselves physically, they become dancers. That's what dance is. Dance is to express a thought or a feeling through movement."

In general, Daniele prefers working on "ensemble" pieces, rather than "star vehicles," and looks to cast actors who can work within the ensemble atmosphere she creates. "[That's] not to say that it [the ensemble] can't include stars, but I think my tendency is to go with the ensemble." At the same time, she recognizes the potential financial security a star can bring to a show. Some productions, she notes, come complete with stars from the outset. "There are cases when the producer comes already with a star [saying], 'We don't do this show without this particular star.'" This can, at times, make the work more difficult, "especially if you don't like the star or don't get along with the star." However, in pieces she creates herself, the ensemble takes precedence over any particular individual. "Because that's what life is about: it's ensemble, it's not about stardom."

Her approach is much more permissive than dictatorial as a director, and she believes "it comes from being Latin, a first-time immigrant, and a woman—which is three minorities—and learning that by screaming I don't get anyplace. So, I learned to be nice. I learned to control my impatience and anger or frustrations and use a very nurturing, calm, seducing [method]. I'm not good enough to be a dictator. I think to be a dictator you have to be so knowledgeable and so brilliant. I think that probably Fosse was a little bit of a dictator, but a benign dictator, because he was very collaborative." She tries to inspire and guide her actors into making discoveries on their own, which gives them not just a sense of ownership "but a sense of process" as well. Rather than make demands of her actors, she has them make demands of themselves. She does this by continuously asking relevant questions of their characters, relationships, motivations, and so forth; working with a system of checks and balances to insure that correct and consistent choices are being made throughout the process. This "open" approach is much more collaborative than authoritative: "I think it's wrong to tell the specialist [the actor], 'You should do this and this and that.'" At the same time, however, she does not ignore her own vision and interpretation of the work. "It's not like I'm permissive in the sense that anybody can do anything they want. As a leader, you must take the responsibility. Every single day you're going to have fifty people or more coming [and] saying, 'Should it be the red shoes, or the yellow shoes?' Or, 'Should I go right or left?' Or, 'Should I cut my hair?' You have to have an answer! You cannot go, 'Oh, well, do whatever you want to.' It would be total chaos. I am talking only about the process. When I get into rehearsal, I know the final destination, but I don't know exactly how the journey's going to be. Therefore, I am quite focused on that final destination, but I allow [for] the improvisation of the journey, because I think it's richer. I just feel like it's going to enrich all of us—it's going to enrich the actors individually, it's going to enrich me, and it's going to enrich mostly the play and the characters."

Although she prefers to go into rehearsals with a completed script and score, she recognizes that the rehearsal process by its very nature often dictates changes that cannot be anticipated until the work gets up on its feet. "Because you learn so much during rehearsals. You think you have the perfect script and then you start rehearsing." She suggests a work can never really be complete until it has been lifted off the page by the actors' interpretation. "Even [with] the greatest writers, you still have the material on the paper. And that's not action, that's not theatre—just paper is not theatre. You have to give it to the actors. You have to have the collaboration of other minds, like designers, directors, choreographers, orchestrators, everybody, who under one vision collaborate in giving ideas. And it doesn't really matter where the ideas come from as long as the baby's perfect." She allows her creative team the freedom during rehearsals to continuously hone, develop, and improve the script and score, looking upon the rehearsal period as not just a process of mounting the show but also as the next step in writing the show.

She finds her ability to read music beneficial throughout this process, for "if you speak in musical terms it's a little faster." However, it is not a skill she believes a director of musicals must possess in order to be effective. "I don't think that you need to *read* music, but I think that you have to have an understanding of the complexities of the musical world, simply because it's easier to speak to the composer and to the musical conductor." Mostly, "I think that you have to *feel* music so well that you can talk with [a] certain assurance about what you want, and why something is not working." Although she has a great deal of performance experience, which she contends helps her as a director, neither does she believe that experience is necessary for all directors.

"I think if a director is understanding of the horrifying process that an actor has to go through . . . then [they] can be perhaps more patient with them, perhaps more nurturing." It is that nurturing quality she brings with her to the rehearsal process.

Daniele allows the uniqueness of each musical to dictate the arrangement of her rehearsal schedule, rather than imposing a standard mode of working on all pieces. Therefore, the beginning of the rehearsal period is purposely unstructured to allow an organic development that draws from the needs of the show and its participants. "The pieces that I have directed in the musical theatre have been so integrated that you don't have to work on the book [first]. If it's necessary to read it, we read it. But it's mostly about creating an atmosphere—as I call it, the Romping Room of the beginning—in which anything is allowable. Up to a certain time in rehearsals, you can do anything you want." Exactly how much time she allows for the freedom of the "Romping Room" remains open, but she suggests that too much time to explore can be counterproductive and that eventually some structure must come to the schedule. Near the end of the rehearsal process her job becomes one of editor. "That's when you come in and say, 'Okay, [these are] three great choices, but you can't do them all.'" Having allowed a freedom to experiment throughout the weeks of rehearsal gives her and the actors multiple points of view from which to choose a single, consistent interpretation.

When it comes to staging (musical staging or blocking), she works simultaneously on two different planes. The first is the educated plane, which intellectually reminds her of staging rules such as "diagonals are stronger than circles," and "staging patterns should not be repeated (unless for effect)." The other is the emotional plane, which creates movement inherent in the soul of the text; here she strives to create "in all of the moments . . . images that mean something. Not images for the sake of images, but images that help [the audience] understand dramatically the moment." She never blocks a scene ahead of time; "I sketch when I have a lot of people on stage that I have to move, but scenes or duets or soli or trios—small things—I sort of leave very loose." Instead she prefers to show the actors "what the world is" by reviewing the set model with them, and then together they work out the actual blocking of the scene. This allows her and her actors freedom to create natural and organic movement with which they all feel comfortable. Overall, the process and exchange between actors and director remains "absolutely free. If I do something that they don't like, or they don't feel is comfortable, they tell me, and it is accepted on the spot. And the same thing: if they make a choice that I feel weakens their character, then I'll tell them and we'll find maybe not my choice, another choice, or maybe a third choice. That's how the process should be, the process that encompasses everybody's work, not just one person." She also "sketches" dances ahead of time, but here again she stops short of staging the entire number prior to rehearsals. "I don't believe in choreographing everything from beginning to end, or staging it from beginning to end. Until you have the people, you can't do it."

For Daniele, the preview period is a critical time. At this stage it becomes crucial to understand what the "final collaborator," the audience, is telling her about the work. The key is knowing "how to listen to them. Even when they are in silence, they are listening. It's extraordinary what their body language and their attention [will tell you]." During her career she has experienced some rocky preview periods: "I know shows that have been fifty percent changed within previews. I have been in shows where the rewrites were every single day." As important as it is to listen to the audience, Daniele believes the director must also listen to the show itself. "If you listen, it tells you. The baby tells you. It starts screaming when it needs help, and it goes fast asleep when it's boring. It's an internal clock that you hear, and the audience does too. You can sense it."

She much prefers out-of-town tryouts to going directly into previews on Broadway. "I think previews in New York can be disastrous. Because New York is like an arena with the lions waiting to eat up the Christians. There's a sense of putting down things here. I don't like that at all." One alternate path available to combat the negative reception granted most New York previews is to mount the show in a workshop prior to a full production. "In a new musical right now with the economics you have to have workshops, because you can't go three months out of town. There's no money. So, the learning process is really with the workshop, when you put everything up and you look at it and *it* tells you what doesn't work. Not only from a directorial point of view" but from an authorship point of view as well.

A good number of the pieces she has done come from regional or nonprofit theatres, although she believes that economics are draining the regional theatre system's effectiveness as a spawning ground for new musicals. "There's no money now. I don't think that the regional theatre ever had too much money or enough money for musicals, because musicals are always so expensive." She would prefer to work more often in regional theatres but admits, "I cannot survive. I cannot feed my stray cat. This is why I have one foot in the regional theatre and the other foot in the commercial theatre which is the one that pays my rent." Even with the limitations of the system, she looks upon it as an invaluable educational resource. "Great people are working in the regional theatres. I've learned a lot working [there]. My heart and my mind and who I am is always in the regional/nonprofit theatre, because that's the one that makes me alive, it makes me create, it makes me dare."

Daniele's busy schedule often demands that once a show has opened she move directly onto her next project. But her role as director does not end on opening night: "They need notes, they need attention, they need care." As a choreographer or as a director she will give notes to the actors "every two months [or] every three months" and will often sit in on a show unannounced. "I copied that from Michael Bennett. He used to appear sometimes, not at the beginning of the show," but after it had already begun. "All of a sudden we'd look and he'd be in the first wing watching," a practice that often sent "a firecracker up your spine" and quickly righted whatever changes may have occurred in the show during the previous weeks. If she has directed a piece, then she will always involve herself in the hiring of cast replacements, which is not necessarily the case if she served as choreographer only.

Although she recognizes the importance of theatre critics in terms of guiding audiences, producers, and investors toward worthwhile productions, she does not read reviews, a lesson she learned from Katherine Hepburn during the Broadway run of *Coco*. Daniele refers to herself as a "visual person," which lends the printed word significant influence over her; thus, detrimental or cruel reviews carry considerable weight that can stop her natural flow of creativity. She also avoids good reviews, which too can wield a strong influence. Overall, she does not believe the artist should be much affected by the words of critics. "An artist is kind of an innocent. We just open the channel and something happens. And hopefully it's going to be something that is right and pleases everybody. But most of the time, the truth of life is that you cannot please everybody. You might please one critic and you might not please the other. But if you start listening—truly listening and believing in that—then what you start doing is closing the channel." Instead, she has others read reviews and inform her as to whether they are generally positive or negative, but she refuses to listen to specifics. "People, especially in America, are extremely governed by the media, and critics, and all that. They have a lot of power on us. So, I have to know if [the reviews] are good, bad, mediocre, whatever. It's the details I'm a little nervous about. Because the detail is what is going to influence me in the next piece to try to please them. I don't want to start directing or choreographing to please one critic, because then the other critic is not going to like it." Pleasing herself and, in turn, pleasing others remain the goals.

For Daniele, the most important aspect of her job as a director "is to be accessible. To everybody. Because the rest is my craft. The rest is what I do: study, research, know what the play's about, have an idea about what the destination is and the process and [the] schedule. I mean, that's the craft. That is expected of any director. But I think that one of the difficult things, when you are in a position of leadership, is to listen to the problems of people." By being accessible, and listening and solving their problems, Daniele strives to motivate her company "so that they create their work one hundred percent, as opposed to seventy percent. I can't talk for anybody else, [but] I feel like when I give myself to a show, the show, the people, everything has the right of asking me. Because I am the leader. It's sort of a maternal kind of leadership: strong but accessible. I don't have children, but it is a very maternal feeling that I feel when I become the director, when I become the leader. I really care. I really truthfully care. And I don't think a mother can tell her children, 'Don't wake up at three o'clock in the morning wanting a glass of water, because I'm not going to be there.' If the kid wants a glass of water, you have to get up and give him a glass of water. You took the responsibility to care for these children for the rest of their lives. We [as directors] don't care for the rest of our lives, but while it lasts, we are responsible.

"I grew up in the dance world, where the behavior of choreographers was extremely neurotic [with] the yelling and insulting; and I thought, 'This is not fun. This is not the way they are getting out of me one hundred percent. This is not the way I am going to be.' I wasn't thinking about when I'm a director, [I was thinking] 'I am not going to be a *human being* like that!' When I am working on something, I want to get up in the morning and look forward to going to rehearsals, work one hundred percent of myself, and come to the end exhausted and say, 'Hey, I can't wait to go back tomorrow!' That's the reason we are in the theatre, I think."

James Lapine

James Lapine never set out to become a Broadway director. The man responsible for such musicals as William Finn's *March of the Falsettos* (1981), and *Falsettoland* (1990; director and co-author); and he and Stephen Sondheim's *Sunday in the Park with George* (1984), *Into the Woods* (1987), and *Passion* (1994) holds a master's degree in photography and design. In the late-'70s he took a job as a design teacher and graphic artist with the Yale School of Drama's *Theater Magazine* and the Yale Repertory Theatre. It was there that he became interested in the theatre.

All quotes are taken from personal interviews conducted by the author with Mr. Lapine.

During Yale's January work month in which teachers and students involve themselves in areas other than their expertise, Lapine's students convinced him to direct. He chose Gertrude Stein's three-page, five-act play, *Photograph*. The transition from photographer to director was not a difficult one for him, for he found the visual orientation similar. "Looking though a viewfinder is not unlike a proscenium itself." *Photograph* provided an opportunity for him to combine his new interest in theatre with his experience and education in photography, allowing him to incorporate a great number of visual elements. "It was called *Photograph* so I used projections. I used projections long before any of these people started using projections in everything." The production, which moved from New Haven to Off Broadway in 1978, garnered Lapine an Obie Award for his directorial debut. "My success came in an instant," he says, a success that surprises him. Ironically, one of the images Lapine projected in his production of *Photograph* was Georges Seurat's nineteenth-century impressionist painting *A Sunday Afternoon on the Island of La Grande Jatte*. "It's an image I've always been fascinated with, so it wasn't unusual, in a way, that I ended up going back to it." It, of course, would become the basis for his first Broadway musical, *Sunday in the Park with George*, for which he received the Pulitzer Prize.

"I had absolutely no training and I don't think you need training," he remarks and points out the irony of a university education in theatre: "Here I was working at Yale as a graphic designer, and there are all these people paying thousands upon thousands of dollars to go learn how to direct and I turn around and have more success than anybody I can remember that was there. So, what does that say?" He is not certain that the university system properly prepares student-directors for the realities of the professional world. "It's great if you can spend three years doing Shakespeare and Chekhov, but you can get out of school and [find] it's not what the opportunities are." His philosophy holds that "people learn by practicing," and not necessarily in the classroom where, using Yale as an example, "a lot of the emphasis is on text analysis."

Lapine believes less attention should be paid to the academic side of directing and more given to the visual and creative aspects. He cites "a good grounding in the visual arts" and a liberal arts education as important tools for the professional director, noting that the individuality of the director's work "comes from the widest breadth of knowledge." Directors whose only frame of reference is the musical theatre Lapine views as "uninteresting," for often their accomplishments tend to be nothing more than an imitation of another director's work. Instead, he believes each director individually should determine their own strengths, then find the type of project that will best illuminate them. Additionally, "I think going and seeing things is very helpful, if you can detach yourself enough from the process of watching the show to break it down," suggesting one learns more from watching a bad production than a good one. "If they're really good you just get lost in it, and you're not [paying attention to what they're doing]. When they're bad, you can sit and analyze why it's bad and figure out what you would have done to make it better."

Although he has no professional performance experience and does not read music (two criteria he feels are unnecessary for a director of musicals), he does consider a musical *understanding* to be critical: "I think if you're not musically inclined you probably shouldn't be directing musicals." He can recognize instantly when someone is singing sharp or flat, or when they are off the beat, and contends that he is musical even though not formally trained. "I hear music, I have a rhythmic sense of life, but I'm not musical in the sense of being able to play anything or read it. Some people are arhythmic, and other people are not. I think you're born tone-deaf or not. I'm fortunate that I was born musical. I can just tell things musically even without an education in it." Overall, he believes the director of a musical must "think rhythmically."

This idea of rhythm is not limited to music. In writing *Sunday in the Park with George*, for instance, Lapine purposely avoided the use of contractions and Latin root words to simulate the rhythmic speech patterns of nineteenth-century France.

He does not consider his lack of education in the theatre a hindrance; on the contrary, he believes it allowed his early work to be more creative and original. Coming in blind, without any frame of reference, he suggests, was to his advantage. "I didn't really know anything about it. I didn't go to the theatre. So, I think it was, in a funny way, my asset, because I didn't have anything to copy. Unfortunately, now I know what I'm doing." Years of work and success on Broadway have given Lapine that education he once lacked, transforming him into an "excellent craftsman," a reality with which he is not entirely delighted. "Frankly, I thought the work was much better when I didn't know what I was doing."

Not having grown up in the theatre, he was never influenced by any of the great Broadway directors of his youth or the well-crafted musicals of the "Golden Age." Though he does not consider himself a postmodernist, he cites his early theatrical exposure and influences as coming from more avant-garde corners of the theatre world, including Robert Wilson, Richard Foreman, and the dance of Meredith Monk. Nowadays his greatest influence comes from his peers in the musical theatre. "They have all influenced me. Because when you go see anybody's work it influences you. Even if you don't necessarily like it, you learn something from it." And there is the issue of accepting the influence of others while keeping one's identity as an artist. "I'm not being coy about it, but there's nobody's work that I've emulated. I haven't really had that strong of an attraction to anybody's work that I wanted to do what they did."

He recognizes a signature quality in his work that differentiates him from others. "You go to Jerry Zaks's shows, they're always very well paced, very well acted, very sleight of hand. You go to Hal's [Prince] shows, they're very visual." Lapine sees his own shows as "very clean and simple. I like to walk a fine line between comedy and drama. I like doing shows like *Into the Woods* that are highly stylized and funny, and sort of turn the tables if you can and make them dark or unsettling. I try to have clarity—a great deal of clarity—in what I do. And I try to not have anything unmotivated, even in a musical," which is inherent in musical theatre of old, but not the type of theatre in which he involves himself. "I'm not likely to direct *Crazy for You* [1992], but I loved *Crazy for You.* But that's something Mike Ockrent does really well. My preference is for a more naturalistic musical theatre so that songs are extensions of dialogue and not relief from dialogue."

Lapine chooses his projects carefully, always seeking material that is "stimulating or challenging for one reason or another. I am not terribly interested in kitchen sink dramas." He has never directed a play or musical that has not interested him; for Lapine, liking the material is a key to its success. However he concedes, "If you're a young director you probably don't always have that choice, but to me, I think you're better off being a waiter," than directing a show that does not interest you.

He particularly enjoys the collaborative process with writers. "What I like about what I do, and I've been very lucky with Bill [Finn] and Steve [Sondheim], is that it's just two of us, so it's very controllable. When I see other shows that have a lyricist, and a composer, and a book writer, and a choreographer, and a director; there are five people in a room—and then a producer—it becomes a battle." Because he is often his own collaborator, he feels that his directorial job is different from most. "I think because I also write it's more unique than the other folks, because I'm envisioning what I'm doing while I'm writing it. I'm not dependent on the writer because I *am* the writer." Juggling the roles of both writer and director is rarely a struggle for Lapine. He finds that, ultimately, wearing both hats is to his advantage. He does, however, prefer the collaborative process (albeit in small groups) to working alone, for it allows him an objectivity toward his work that is more difficult to achieve when writing and directing a play. The camaraderie contributes another set of eyes and ears off of which to bounce ideas and upon which he relies to insure his own are being realized on stage.

Although he believes the director can be very influential in the writing of a show if on board from the outset, he does not necessarily believe he should be the final editor of the script and score: "We're all there to serve the writer." He concedes, however, there are times when the writers refuse a director's guidance. "Often you can tell when the writers are running the show versus the director . . . stuff needs to be cut and it's not." Sometimes, however, Lapine believes a director just has to put his foot down and make demands for the good of the show. "The nice thing about the theatre is you can cut a number or a song [and] the audience won't know it's missing. And if it doesn't work you can put it back in. When the authors dig in their heels and say, 'I won't change a thing!' they're just shooting themselves in the foot." The shaping and molding a director can offer a writer's work can be substantial, and yet he knows where the line is drawn between collaborating and dominating. "I don't like going to shows where the direction calls such attention to itself, or [when] you get a sense that directors don't trust the material so they feel they have to embellish it." Even on shows where he is not publicly credited with authorship, such as *March of the Falsettos*, the director's hand is subtly at work in the writing: "I did help write it, even though I didn't have spoken words in it." All in all, he admits that the collaborative process basically boils down to passion. "I think that, in a way, creating a musical has a lot to do with power. Generally people who feel strongest about a certain aspect of what's going on will win out by virtue of the fact that they're most passionate about it. And I don't think that's a bad thing."

When it comes to working with actors, Lapine sees himself as far more collaborative than dictatorial. "I know there are certain directors who say, 'Go do this. Do it like that,'" he says, and admits there are some actors who prefer being told exactly what to do, but that is not Lapine's style. He enjoys the give-and-take with the ensemble of actors and looks upon his role of director as being "the captain of the team." He admits that when he first began directing he did not know how to talk to actors. "It was hard for me to articulate. And when I started *writing* and directing I heard a language in my head and I kept trying to get the actors to do it the way I heard it." Now, with that obstacle behind him, Lapine stresses, "You just have to justify what you ask an actor to do. You have to have a reason to do it, even if [the reason is] 'It's boring over there,' or 'nobody can see you,' or 'that's not a strong position on the stage.' You have to be able to justify your choices in a way that people can make sense of them and not feel like a robot."

In addition to musicals, Lapine has directed a number of straight plays (most notably a 1997 revival of *The Diary of Anne Frank* and David Henry Hwang's *Golden Child*). His approach to directing both plays and musicals is much the same: "I think that's a fallacy to think you do them necessarily differently." However, he contends that musicals on the whole usually demand a different style of acting and a different style of presentation than a play. Defining that style and obtaining the correct performances from the actors are just two of the director's jobs. It's a matter of "giving them the scale of the performance. All actors come in with different styles of training. If you've done commedia del'arte and you've done French farce, you can do a heightened reality for a musical. There's no reason why anybody can't do both." That scale varies, Lapine notes, from musicals, to plays, to film and television. "Musicals, as a whole, tend to play much bigger houses than plays. So, [the actors are] used to having to exaggerate a little bit more just for the sake of [the house size]." On the other hand, when Lapine and company approached filming *Passion* for public television's *American Playhouse*, he conducted a special daylong rehearsal to "scale it to the camera. We rehearsed it as a movie and just brought everything down. And it works just dandy."

In pre-production, Lapine sees designing the set as the director's most difficult job, "because you have to be so theoretical. You have to imagine your production before you've gotten to rehearse it, so you have to be very careful that you don't design something that you're going to regret in two months once you're in the rehearsal hall." He usually comes into a show with very strong opnions abouts its scenic design, a disposition he attributes to his design background. "I find most set designers really love that. They love having a director who really has a sense of what [he] want[s]." His sense and understanding of costumes, however, is more limited. Here he must rely more heavily on his designers, which in some cases can be difficult. "Costume sketches can be very tricky [to read]. They can look great and end up to be ugly costumes, because all you get is the little swatch." This is made even more frustrating for him by the fact that "there are some costume designers who are wonderful artists [when it comes to renderings], but in the end are not great designers. And then there are other designers who can't draw worth shit."

In terms of the design, he always tries to give himself as much flexibility as possible, particularly in musicals. With musical numbers invariably coming and going during rehearsals, Lapine likes sets that are designed to allow for slight variances and changes unanticipated at the outset. "Every show I've done there have been scenic things I've needed after the fact, so you have to leave yourself a little room for that. I've seen shows which have been prisoners to their set. You want to design a set that's flexible so that you don't get cornered." He suggests that the European style of play production may be more appropriate. "European directors rehearse for four to six months, and they're able to not have to design their sets until after they've already gotten into the rehearsal hall. It's a much smarter way to work, but we don't have that luxury here."

Ultimately, however, Lapine's greatest focus during pre-production is on casting. Conducting auditions is not something he looks forward to and he admits that the most difficult aspect of the long process is staying alert, finding that it is easy to "zone out." Generally, he looks for "people who are kind of interesting and alive, and who can maybe bring more to the material than is there," as opposed to actors who "nail the role on the spot" at the audition. He is wary of such actors because often they "never get any better, and by the time they get on stage after six weeks are stale." At the same time, he acknowledges, that "each project requires a different kind of performer. Sometimes, if you're doing a reading, you *want* somebody who can nail it and doesn't need a lot of rehearsal. Other times, when you're going to be doing a project for two years, it's more fun to take a chance on somebody who has interesting qualities that you can mold the role around."

When casting a play, he suggests a good actor is always the best choice for a role, even if they are not the ideal "type" the director originally had in mind. When directing a musical, however, he more often than not will hire a singer over an actor. "In a musical I opt for the singer, if it's a star singing part, because you have to trust yourself as an actor to make it work. But an actor that doesn't really sing that well I find hard to listen to in a show. People come to musicals to hear people sing, they don't come to hear them talk, per se." Of course, he always hopes to find both qualities in one person. He also looks for actors who are adaptable and flexible. At auditions he will often give actors improvisations or other unexpected tests to reveal an actor's versatility, character, and range. "I sort of throw curve balls at actors when they audition because I like to see if they're game. And some aren't, you know. I remember [quite a talented] actress saying to me, 'I don't feel comfortable rewriting your play.' And I thought, 'Well, then she's not somebody I want to work with.' And other people just get off on that. So, it's chemistry."

In addition to casting talent, Lapine takes personality into consideration as he always tries to cast a company that's compatible. He strives to create an ensemble that can not only work together, but also play together. Reputation, as well, plays into his decision-making process. He is reluctant to work with actors who have a history of being difficult to work with, or who are not "company" people, or who are "divas." "Often, if that's the case, I'll confront the person before I hire them and say, 'Look, let's talk about this. This may not be true, but this is what I hear. This is how I work. And if you don't feel comfortable with that, you probably shouldn't do it.'" Sometimes, however, for all the time, patience, and care he puts into casting, mistakes do happen. In those cases he feels it is best to replace the person. "I've fired a number of people. I think you can't be wimpy about those things." He also admits that "there are people I should've fired that I haven't." This, he believes, is not only a disservice to the show but also to the performer: "You're not doing the actor any favors if they're not doing the show."

He recognizes the drawing power and financial stability big-name stars bring to the commercial theatre: "If you look at the grosses it really seems to make a big difference if you've got somebody recognizable in it. [And] I think for people from out of town, the excitement of the theatre is being in the same room as Christopher Plummer or Bernadette Peters. It makes it a little more special." He is uncertain, however, as to whether all shows benefit from a drawing personality. *Passion*, for example, he does not believe would have had a longer run had it name stars heading the cast. "I think *Passion* was a show that belonged Off Broadway or in an opera house and not in the commercial Broadway theatre. It had a limited audience, a limited run. It had its fans and its detractors. It was different. No song really culminated in a hand. It had no intermission. It didn't fit into the mold of the usual Broadway show."

Lapine feels that if, during pre-production, the director designs the production (sets and costumes) intelligently, casts the show carefully and properly, and picks the most suitable theatre to display the piece, by the time he or she moves into rehearsals a majority of the work is done. Or, to sum it up more succinctly: "Someone said, 'Directing is what you do prior to getting into the first rehearsal.'" What is not a top priority for Lapine during pre-production is the completion of the script and score. "Most of the shows I do are half-written" by the time rehearsals begin. He clarifies, "I wouldn't want to do a Broadway show that way," but he thinks it is "sort of exciting" when developing a piece in a workshop to not necessarily have all the questions answered at the outset. "I know in the *Falsetto* shows we went in with incomplete scripts and it was sort of exciting. But the thing is the stakes weren't as high, particularly on the first one. Sometimes it helps to be in the process to know how to finish doing the writing."

He rarely works with a choreographer and stages most of his own musical numbers. "It doesn't mean that somebody [else] wouldn't have done a better job with it, but I have to say I enjoy doing it myself." When he does work with a choreographer the process is collaborative: "Often what I do is sketch it in, and then the choreographer will come in and take it over. Or sometimes the choreographer will have a game plan before we go in." There is "no rule of thumb," according to Lapine, who believes that each project should find its own form. Once the form of the work is defined, then a division of labor among the collaborators can be enacted to accommodate the specific requirements of that show. Yet Lapine's choreographers are by no means limited to chore-ography. "The choreographers I've liked working with are the ones that you talk to about the book, you talk to about the direction, you talk to about performance. It's not necessarily limited to this person only doing movement. I really look to them for feedback on other areas of the production."

Of the usual five-week rehearsal period, he has learned to let "the first week or week and a half be very much about the actors. Every actor's different. Some actors come in with a lot of homework done and they want to try a lot of things that they've thought about. Other actors will want to know exactly what you're looking for the minute they start rehearsals." Rather than define exactly how he sees the piece, he prefers to see in that first week what the actors will bring to the material. In addition, "I find you always get actors that come from different schools of training; some actors are giving you one hundred percent the first day, other actors are marking things. I feel you have to let a little bit of chaos ensue in the first week or so, so everybody's method can kind of be met for a while. And then I kick in, in a much more intense way to pull it to a place that I want it to go." He concedes, "I'm not a big table person. A lot of directors like to sit around a table and really concentrate on the writing. I like to get things on their feet."

The staging of the show is often mapped out prior to rehearsals. "When I first started directing, I always used a grid pattern and I did all my blocking on paper, and worked on a model, and generally I had things pretty well worked out before I came into rehearsal." Though he approaches some shows in a more relaxed manner, choosing to work out the blocking with the actors (primarily straight plays), more often than not when directing a musical he continues to pre-block his shows before working with the company. This allows him to work quickly. At the end of every week of rehearsal, including the first, he likes to hold a run-through of the entire show. Sometimes at these run-throughs, actors find themselves "performing" scenes they have never even rehearsed up to that point. In those cases, Lapine still asks the actors to "get up and move around," and utilize the stage space. Although he acknowledges that "a lot of actors are really uncomfortable doing that," it allows him to look at the overall production and avoid getting caught up in trivial particulars. "Then I'll start in on all the detail work again the next week."

In addition to defining and staging the show and giving the actors the scale of the performance, Lapine always takes time during the rehearsal period to rehearse the actors through the songs without musical accompaniment. "I always have them speak the lyrics and act the lyrics. [I have them] do the show without music so that the lyrics don't get locked to the notes in a way that they don't know what they're singing, [and just end up] singing songs. So that the songs have real impact as *plot*." He believes that each song should tell a story, not be a respite from it. "I find it's a great exercise and it really helps the singer stay in character when they sing." Overall, he enjoys the energy and excitement rehearsals bring to a production and remains open to new and better ideas during the rehearsal process. At the same time, he is careful to avoid being overwhelmed by the work. "The worst thing is to be entrenched," for once the director is in over his or her head, the creative process ends.

In general, he would prefer opening his Broadway shows on the road, but does not always have that luxury. He admits that *Sunday in the Park with George*, his first Broadway production, did not play out of town primarily due to his inexperienced belief that its original Playwrights Horizons workshop production was sufficient preparation for Broadway. With his next show, *Into the Woods*, his attitude changed. He feels the production benefited greatly from its original regional production at the Old Globe Theatre in San Diego. "But with *Passion* we didn't go out of town and we really should have." Lapine regards previewing on Broadway as a hindrance, suggesting that some shows worked on and revised in front of the New York public receive such bad word-of-mouth based on early reports that "it's almost impossible to overcome" the negative reputation they acquire. He points to

Titanic (1997), the Maury Yeston/Peter Stone epic musical that overcame bad press to ultimately win the Tony Award for best musical of the year, as being the exception, rather than the rule. Time constraints and other considerations often dictate the way in which a show previews. "*Passion* I was just really anxious to get up," for, among other reasons, "to make the Tony deadline." And, in fact, *Passion* did win the Tony for best musical in 1995. Although he has little interest in the Tony Nominating Committee's agenda, he acknowledges, "If you win a Tony Award it gives the show a little more life outside the New York area."

Lapine is careful to distance himself slightly from the production once it goes into previews. "I don't go to every preview. For me, I lose my objectivity if I'm there [all] eight performances a week in previews. So, I'll generally take a couple off [and] send an assistant. Invariably they always have good shows when I'm not there." He also implies that the director's absence provides a healthy freedom to a show: "The actors like to know that I'm not always there." He works in the same manner when working cast replacements into a show. "I heard Jerry [Zaks] was there for every preview of Whoopi's. [Goldberg was Nathan Lane's replacement as Pseudolus in Zaks's 1996 revival of *A Funny Thing Happened on the Way to the Forum*]. I could never do that."

Following the show's opening, Lapine's job as director is not over. On average, he likes to sit in on a performance "once every couple of weeks" to insure the production does not evolve in unintended directions. When not in attendance he relies on "a stage manager who knows how to contain a show." If he is available, Lapine will also involve himself in cast replacements during the run of the show and will often, at that time, go back into rehearsal with the entire company to brush up aspects of the show that have weakened over time.

For Lapine, the difference between directing existing material and developing new material is considerable. "It's much easier to direct a show after you've seen it. It's very easy to go see a show and [think], 'I don't know why they did *that*, I'll do *this*.' You don't have that luxury when you're in the middle of it and you've already designed the set and you're stuck with it and it cost a half a million dollars and now you've made a mistake and you have to make it work." The irony of it being, "Often my shows will get reviewed after the fact when somebody's done a production somewhere and I get these great reviews."

Lapine has developed for himself a clear understanding of the director's role. "Casting is the most crucial aspect of what you do. No matter how good a show you have, if you don't have the right people in it, it's not going to fly." Following that he focuses on designing the show, "because you have to let the audience know what the show is, what the style of it is, what the world of it is. And if you get that wrong it can be a huge obstacle to getting involved in the show." And if it is an original piece, he believes the job description includes, "being there for the writers and helping them get it right. Making their work work is the first thing, and that's sort of part and parcel [of] casting." The director must be confident and "bold-stroked" with his or her attitude toward the production. Nothing is too precious to be changed—the director cannot cling to aspects of the show that do not work. "I did a Shakespeare show that was almost single-handedly ruined by the costumes, but they cost so much money I couldn't even fathom getting rid of them. But I learned my lesson." Ultimately, for Lapine, the job of directing boils down to one simple idea: "Tell a story. That's all. That's all there ever is. Plays, movies, musicals, you have to tell a story. It's that simple."

Over the years, Lapine's style as a director has matured, giving him a confidence with which he is comfortable. His unexpected career, however, is still evolving. "Because I started in graphic design, it's all been sort of a lark, and I keep waiting for it to be over. I don't relish [the successes] too much. I try and keep it in perspective."

Arthur Laurents

Arthur Laurents began life in the theatre as a playwright and book writer responsible for such musicals as *West Side Story* (1957), *Gypsy* (1959), *Anyone Can Whistle* (1964), *Do I Hear a Waltz?* (1965; based on his play *The Time of the Cuckoo*), *Hallelujah, Baby!* (1967), and *Nick and Nora* (1991). He began directing "because there were very few directors I thought were any good." His initial outing resulted in the Harold Rome musical *I Can Get It for You Wholesale* (1962), followed by he and Stephen Sondheim's *Anyone Can Whistle*, Jerry Herman's *La*

All quotes are taken from personal interviews conducted by the author with Mr. Laurents.

Cage aux Folles (1983; for which he received a Tony Award), the Strouse/Maltby musical *Nick and Nora* (1991), and two noteworthy revivals of *Gypsy*: the first starring Angela Lansbury (1974), the second with Tyne Daly (1989).

Once he had made the decision to pursue directing, he says, "I went around to a great many acting classes. I think very few directors, then and now, know anything about acting. Acting is just as important in a musical. Most directors of musicals are choreographers and, in my opinion, cannot direct actors, because a choreographer works with bodies, not with human beings who think and have ideas of their own. An actor can be creative and bring things to a part, [yet] the choreographer is saying, 'Do it like this—with the pinky!'" For Laurents, the acting in a musical should not cease once the music begins, and he gets frustrated with directors who allow their actors to just "stand there and sing a song. They're just singing. It's a glorious voice, but to me it's boring. What are they singing *about*? What are they feeling? Of course, very few people can write lyrics like Steve [Sondheim], but you can fake it; you can make it seem like there's more there if they're acting something. But you have to give them something to act. That's my strong point; I know how to direct actors. And that's something most directors don't do."

Laurents credits director Elia Kazan with having the greatest influence on his work as a director. "He was a marvelous director. He made plays exciting through the acting." Laurents took that idea and applied it to the musical theatre. He also believes attending the theatre is beneficial: "I saw theatre from the time I was ten years old. I think we learn mostly by going and seeing." Laurents acted only briefly in nightclubs early in his career, but he does not think directors need performance experience to be successful at their craft. And though he does not read music, he has an innate understanding of it: "Leonard Bernstein and Steve Sondheim say I have an incredible ear. I can't tell you a diminished fifth from a whatever-it-is, but I can hear. And I can hear what, at least to me, sounds right and what doesn't. It's like anything else: there is a natural, inexplicable something called talent, and that is necessary to do first-rate work of any kind. You can't learn that. As it says in *Gypsy*: 'You either got it or you ain't.'" Although talent can't be learned, Laurents believes "you can develop it" and points to the Neighborhood Playhouse and Juilliard (both located in New York City) as two noteworthy training programs. Of most other college and university programs in the United States, however, Laurents remains suspect: "They [the students] may get their M.F.A.s but they don't know anything about theatre."

He does not feel young directors seeking experience should limit their opportunities by only taking on shows that interest them. "I didn't like [*I Can Get It For You*] *Wholesale* very much. David Merrick asked me to do it, and I wanted to direct a musical. And I thought, 'Well, he's giving me an opportunity, and I'm going to see what I can do with it.'" He admits now that as his career progressed, he felt it necessary to have an emotional connection with a show in order to be effective: "The reason why [*Nick and Nora*] didn't work was my fault. There's only one reason to direct or to write, and that is because you care. I didn't care enough." He took on the directorial reins of that show as a favor for a friend ("a terrible mistake"), and later took over as author after the original writer was released. Ultimately, he believes the problem with the show lay in the concept to musicalize *The Thin Man* films in the first place. "The fundamental mistake was that Nick and Nora Charles don't exist. Not in Dashiell Hammett—not anyplace. They are Myrna Loy and William Powell [the film's stars], and no matter who you cast, that's who the audience sees."

Though he has worn the hat of playwright more often than that of director, he contends, "Somebody has to make the final decision. There can only be one captain of the ship and that has to be the director." With that, playwright Laurents relinquishes the final editorial power of his plays and musicals to the director; and when he is directing, he expects his writers to do the same. As a director, Laurents has never gone into rehearsals without a completed script and score and says he never will. "Changes are going to happen anyway," and those changes are difficult enough without having the added burden of completing the initial draft in rehearsals. "I began as the director of a musical called *The Rink* [1984; eventually directed on Broadway by A. J. Antoon]. And they wanted to go into rehearsal and I said it wasn't ready." The creative team disagreed with Laurents's recommendation and began rehearsals nonetheless. "And the show was no good. And it *could* have been, but it wasn't ready." This is not an isolated case, according to Laurents. "People are too eager to push something into rehearsal before it's ready." The problem, he suggests, is "they don't want to do any more work. The reason for these failures is they get started and they can't stop. Everybody says, 'We've invested time, we've invested money. Keep going.' They keep going and land in the abyss." Additionally, he points out that shows discovered to need "a whole reworking" once rehearsals have begun are destined for failure and should be aborted. "You're kidding yourself. It's got cancer; there's no chemo to cure it."

His instinct for editing a script and score is just that, an instinct. "You can only go by sensing it." During rehearsals of *La Cage aux Folles*, for example, he recalls, "I thought, 'There's a big hole in the second act. We don't have enough music.'" That recognition and intuitive feel for structure led to the incorporation of an additional song, "Cocktail Counterpoint," which was used in the show as a vehicle to pull the two families together. The addition of music for Laurents may begin as an instinct toward structure, but he feels it must also serve a function in the context of the story; an obvious, but often overlooked, assertion. "I don't say it has to advance the plot, but it has to do something emotionally."

Laurents has written most of the musicals that he has directed. Nevertheless, he generally does not think it a good idea for authors to direct their own works. "I think it helps to have another take on it." Earlier in his career he often relied on the judgment of a knowledgeable and creative producer for that objectivity, but no longer. "Now, if there were producers who were more than moneymen I wouldn't say that. But one of the biggest lacks in the theatre today is the producer. You always need somebody who has an allover view, as opposed to the people actively working on it. Somebody who stands back and says, 'Is this what you're trying to do? Because this is what I see.' Well, if you are the director and the author, and you don't have a producer, there's nobody. There always has to be somebody to say 'but . . . ' If you don't have that, you're in trouble. If everyone's running around saying, 'It's wonderful, it's wonderful,' you're in for a rude awakening, because it's never that wonderful." Even people who call themselves producers, however, are not necessarily qualified for the job. Laurents first discovered this frustrating reality in Philadelphia during the out-of-town tryout for *Anyone Can Whistle*. "The producer [Kermit Bloomgarden] said, 'There is someone's opinion I'd really like you to listen to.' I said, 'I'd be glad to.' It was his sixteen-year-old son! And [Bloomgarden's] partner was a woman [Diana Krasny] who said, 'You must change Lee Remick's dress. The color is all wrong.' As if *that* was going to make or break the show. They're not producers."

When directing his own work, Laurents finds it easy to separate the two jobs of writer and director. On his revivals of *Gypsy*, he says, "Both times I had no consciousness that I wrote it. You're removed from it." On both occasions he found himself cutting the script to accommodate the production. "And I would like to have cut more, but I didn't. The thing was too good." This ability to understand the roles of both the director and author—where they overlap, where they are different, and how the two work together—has made a tremendous difference to him working with other writers and composers. However, this was not evident to him at the outset of his directing career. During his first show, *I Can Get It for You Wholesale*, for instance, he "had a not-too-pleasant learning experience. Since I was an author I thought, 'I'm going to be true to the authors. I'm not going to be like these other directors and push them around.' Well, we opened in Philadelphia; the show got panned. They said, 'Oh yes, we'll rewrite,' and they rewrote, and it was no good. So, I stepped in," and began making decisions from a director's point of view.

Laurents admits he is a somewhat dictatorial director, "to a point. I think you lead them, then you give them a little play in the rein," to stimulate creativity in the cast and allow them to contribute, "then you pull it in," to bring about a unified production. He approaches directing straight plays in the same fashion. "The difference is in a musical [the performers] are so surprised that anybody treats them that way [like serious actors] that they give you *more*. They expect to be told, 'Go here, go there, sing out Louise.'" He admits that early in his directing career if an actor did something on stage that had not been prompted by him, he would think, "'Well, I didn't ask him or her to do that. What are they doing that for?' Then I had to face the fact that what they were doing was very good. 'So,' [I thought,] 'just shut up and let them do it.' A director by nature is a control freak, [but] you have to be flexible." He believes when musicals are approached with the same "three-dimensional" goals as straight plays, the payoff is greater. "Most musicals are two-dimensional. Sometimes [the characters are] written in an uninteresting manner, but you can find ways to trick it, and make it at least *seem* interesting. I don't mean by giving them ticks, but you give them a subtext, and [the results are] amazing." Laurents sees this subtext as the key: "If the actor is really thinking something, the audience will get it—no matter what he's saying. That makes directing fun, and I know it makes it fun for the actors." In *La Cage aux Folles*, for example,

Laurents incorporated a subtext for the song "Masculinity" to create a very strong number from a relatively weak song. "[The song] became too jokey. There was no reality. It wasn't funny enough to let it go at that, and it needed some underpinning. I told all these guys who were supposed to be tough, and George Hearn who was the leading character [Albin], 'This was like being a kid, and the other kids called you faggot!' I told them to act like that to him." From that premise, Albin was challenged to win them over during the course of the song, which he did. "It became very moving because of that. It was in line with the theme of the show [and] gave texture to something that was [before just a] comedy song."

Above all else, Laurents strives for truth in his storytelling. "Under everything there's an emotional reality. I think that's essential in all theatre. That is the core for me, the whole theory behind it." He seeks this emotional reality in the writing, the scenery, even the dances. "When we did *West Side Story*, before we went into rehearsal, Jerry Robbins [the director-choreographer] said to me, 'I can't do "The Prologue."' I said, 'Why?' He said, 'I don't know what it's about.' So, I wrote a scenario—what those gangs were doing, and why, and what they were thinking and feeling. Well, that may sound a little pretentious because they were dancing, but it informed the whole thing and gave it this emotional reality." Laurents was in on the writing of *La Cage aux Folles* from the beginning as a director, and as with his own emotional reality-based writing, he kept the piece focused by continually asking one question: "What is it about? What is *La Cage aux Folles* about? It's about a boy who has to accept a man as his mother. That's what it's about. And when you start there, that informs the whole piece and makes it rather easy to do. All the feathers, and sequins, and camp, and all that. . . . It comes down to a boy who has to accept a man as his mother. That's the story you're telling."

Laurents's approach to directing musicals includes what he calls "'the schmear.' That's the theatrical exterior," a heightened element of theatricality that he excludes from his straight plays. "Unfortunately, it fools too many people into thinking they're seeing something." Regarding shows such as *Cats* (1982), *Phantom of the Opera* (1988), and *Miss Saigon* (1991) he insists, "They're all about scenery. Where are the meat and potatoes?" He believes there is a fine line that must be walked between adding "theatrical" elements (which he advocates) and creating productions that *rely* on scenic spectacle for their enter-tainment value. "Don't take a musical and try to overdress it. Use scenery that will bring out what the piece is. I remember I had a scenic idea for *The Rink* [the Kander and Ebb musical set in a roller skating rink]. There was a song they had called 'Colored Lights,' and I wanted to begin the show with that, and show what they *thought* the rink was. And then you see it as the shabby nothing [it really is]. That is theatri-cal, but again, there's the emotional reality. There's a reason. They're theatrical ideas, but they give an emotional kick and underline the point." He believes this theatricality at the beginning of a piece helps draw the audience in and establishes the show's style. The opening for *La Cage aux Folles*, for example, which revealed the streets of St. Tropez before slowly evolving into the La Cage aux Folles nightclub, was technically elaborate. In fact, the opening preview performance had to be canceled because it did not work. "Technically it was a bitch, but it was worth doing because it made the thing theatrical. Right away it said, 'We are taking you into the theatre.'" Thus, even though there is a theatricality to Laurents's work, which invites patrons into the the-atre's world of illusion, he insists on an emotional reality within the context of the play itself.

For Laurents there is no denying "the two most essential elements: character (the most essential element in any kind of theatre), and then style (how you tell it)." He warns that a show lacking in character and style more often than not will end up being "boring," something he considers "a cardinal sin. It's okay to be bad, but not to be boring." As important as style is to him, he admits a show cannot be dictated by style alone. "I think content determines form," meaning the subject matter of the show itself defines its style (or the way in which the story is told). When he and Stephen Sondheim sat down to write *Anyone Can Whistle* they were aware that it was "very experimental," but they never set out to intentionally break the rules. What they discovered was "this is what the material called for."

During pre-production, Laurents believes the director's main focus should be on the scenery. "It's the first thing they see. It really sets the style." He regrets that the use of the main curtain is today frequently eliminated. "To me, one of the great thrills of the theatre: you walk in, there's a curtain. What's going to be behind it?" Without the curtain "you *see* what's behind it. It takes away the surprise. And the theatre is surprise." He actively involves himself in the design of the scenery for his shows; though rather than come in with strong ideas of what the scenery should be, he comes in with "ideas of what it should *do,*" emotionally as well as physically. "How to do it, I don't have a clue. I count on the designers for that." Sometimes, however, designs go awry. For *I Can Get It for You Wholesale*, "I wanted all the scenery black, white, and gray, but in each scene a different slash of color: the scene in the nightclub, a big red slash; the kitchen, pale blue. Something like that. Well, [David] Merrick, who produced it, his favorite color was red. And the designer was trying to please Merrick *and* trying to please me; and everything came out pink! It was ghastly. We had terrible battles. I didn't entirely win. Nobody did. That's the problem: where nobody wins, everybody loses." He points to clear and constant communication between the designer and director throughout the build process as being the key. "You're not there when they're putting the paint on it." When the set arrives at the theatre, all questions should already have been answered, because at that point it is usually too late to make great

changes. There are times, he admits, when wonderful scenic contributions happen by luck. "In *West Side Story* when the streamers come
down [during 'The Dance at the Gym'], that was an accident. It happened during technical rehearsal." The streamers for the number were
supposed to be in place by the time the lights came up; but they came
in by accident (luck) after the scene was established, with lights up, in
full view of the audience. "Everybody said, 'Keep it in!' That was one of
the most stunning effects of the show."

Laurents often works with the same designers from project to project, as he has with lighting designer Jules Fisher and costume designer Theoni V. Aldredge. "Trust" in their work is the reason. This trust
is based on their in-depth working knowledge of their crafts beyond
mere design abilities. For example, regarding Aldredge's technical
skills, Laurents exclaims: "She can *sew*! She knows how to sew and
cut, which makes a big difference. She knows how it will fit and move,"
an understanding a good number of designers lack.

Choosing the right theatre is another important directorial decision,
though one which often has tremendous limitations attached to it. "The
size of the theatre, that's very important. But you rarely have a choice,"
due mainly to the availability of Broadway houses at the time a show
comes to town. For his Tyne Daly revival of *Gypsy*, he states, "By luck
we got the St. James Theatre. *Gypsy* is really a musical play about four
people. Anything else is set dressing. You need a fairly intimate theatre.
The St. James's auditorium is small, and you're right there with those
four people. So, the play worked wonderfully. To go into a bigger theatre, we'd be in trouble."

"Hands down," casting is the most important job the director performs. "If it's cast right, fifty percent of your work is done. [But] if you
haven't got the right actor," the show will not work, even if the actor you
have is quite competent. Laurents points to one startling example:
Hallelujah, Baby! "I was very, very close with Lena Horne. I wrote it for

her. And then she pulled out. The show should have been stopped, because it was written for Lena." Instead, Leslie Uggams was signed on to play the lead role of Georgina. "Leslie Uggams is adorable. She's one of the nicest women I've ever met in the theatre," but she was not the "angry, bitchy lady" Laurents had written. The writers "tried to adjust it" to Uggams's talents, but ultimately they only succeeded in diluting the impact of the piece. "That was another show [with Uggams in the role]." Too many compromises, all prompted by an incorrect casting choice, resulted in a show that proved unsatisfying to him. Ironically, Leslie Uggams received the Tony Award for best actress in a musical for her performance that year (tied with Patricia Routledge in *Darling of the Day*).

"Casting really is the most important thing. That determines everything. It even determines the morale of the company, and how you direct them." Laurents admits not all casting choices are pleasant ones, having knowingly cast some actors with poor reputations because they were right for the role. "You know [they're] going to be a pain in the ass, but okay. He or she is worth it." He tends to cast people based on talent and contends he has never cast someone on name alone. He acknowledges that "stars are an enormous help in selling tickets," but thinks there are fewer stars than producers would have you believe: "There are people who are supposed stars, but they don't sell a ticket." He does think stars are a necessity "if you write something with a strong central character as in *Gypsy*, for example. The only person who can play it is a star because that's going to be the person who has the experience and the skill and the craft." In general, however, "I don't think you need them if the work is good." Laurents is also an advocate of color-blind casting and applauds shows such as *Rent* (1996) and *The Life* (1997), not only for the directors' integrated casting practices but for the writers' choices to integrate the characters on the pages of their scripts.

With casting being the director's single most significant task, it is not surprising that Laurents finds the audition process to be very important. He believes it is vital to audition a performer more than once, suggesting that at a first audition, "you can tell whether they're a 'possible,'" but at a second audition you discover whether they are right for the role. "You can be fooled that they're a possible by a very flashy [first] audition. I mean, they may be good, but they may be all wrong [for the role]. So, you have to have them back to see." At his auditions he very often asks the performers "to try something that is not exactly what's written." Frequently he has them play the scene "from a different viewpoint" in order to assess their skill level and range. This technique can sometimes net unexpected treasures. "There was a part in *La Cage aux Folles*: Jacqueline [played on Broadway by Elizabeth Parrish], this woman who ran this nightclub. I didn't know what in God's name she was. I kept hoping *somebody* would come in. And this woman came in, and I could see something. I said, 'Listen, never mind what's there [in the script]. Just tell me who she is.' Well, suddenly she became this crazed person, and I thought, 'Great!' It didn't matter what she said. I didn't know what was going on in her head, but it was fascinating! I was saved and it came from an audition."

Laurents works closely with a casting director "in whom I have a lot of faith," to whittle down the group of prospective cast members before he sees them. "I'm not going to sit for days, because you go deaf, dumb, and blind, and you lose any judgment." He does not feel that a casting director limits his possibilities nor eliminates finding that diamond in the rough: "You have to trust other people." One of those diamonds Laurents discovered was Barbra Streisand. At age nineteen, "she just came in and auditioned. When she started to sing I thought I would die. I was thrilled with that voice and just kept her singing." He eventually cast her in the comedic role of Miss Marmelstein in *I Can Get It for You Wholesale*. "The part was a fifty-year-old spinster. So, I said to the authors, 'She's obviously a spinster, what difference does the age make?'"

Laurents finds the rehearsal schedule for a musical to be an important yet difficult element to work out. "You have to balance it so that the music and the book and the dancing get enough time. And that's not easy." He notes that his rehearsal schedule changes from show to show depending upon each show's distribution of music, dancing, and book scenes, and subsequently the demands on the actor's time. Once in rehearsal, Laurents works quickly. "In a musical I start putting it on its feet the second day (wouldn't with a play). Not in any rigid blocking, but some kind of idea. Because it gives them [the actors] a chance to feel their way around, and know what the stage is going to be like." From that a director can begin to see the picture evolve. "The sooner you have, first, the scene, and then the act on its feet, the sooner you can tell if the shape of the whole piece is right." That, he believes, is something the director should "find out early on."

He does not pre-block his shows, nor does he go about blocking every show in the same manner. Sometimes he has strong visual ideas he wants to incorporate, while other times he prefers to work out the staging with the actors. What he strives for most is motivated blocking that is appropriate to the scene and the characters involved. "When I directed *I Can Get It for You Wholesale* there was a scene where a man came in who had been a fink and betrayed everybody. When he entered everyone on stage turned their backs to him. It was a very effective moment." But it was not just an effect, or movement for the sake of movement (two blocking mistakes Laurents believes audiences find either consciously or unconsciously "distracting")—there was a reason for it. "In *Gypsy* there is a hotel room scene where all these kids have to run around. I finally realized the only way to stage it was to give them a reason for going where they did. When they have a reason it is always much more effective blocking." He also works hard to eliminate arbitrary movement that is inconsistent with each individual character. Additionally, there are times when no movement at all is the most effective choice. "I think [directors] are very often afraid to just let the actor sit or stand, and just do it [act]. Most directors today are carried away with themselves. They do a lot of fancy staging, a lot of multimedia stuff, but they don't get to the actor. And I think the actor is the essence of the performance."

He enjoys staging his own musical numbers ("songs where they just sing"), but "if it comes to any kind of real movement, I don't know how to do it, and I'd let the choreographer do it." Depending upon the number, Laurents will turn entire songs over to the choreographer if at some point the piece requires dance. For instance, the number "With Anne on My Arm," from *La Cage aux Folles*, which begins as a conversational solo and then evolves into a rather elaborate dance number, Laurents says, "I turned the whole number over to him [Scott Salmon, choreographer]."

One of the rehearsal techniques Laurents likes to incorporate comes three to four weeks into the process, once he feels the actors have a handle on the lines and the blocking: "I have everybody sit around the table and act their lines," including lyrics (without musical accompaniment). "It gives them a sense of what the whole show is, [and] of what they're playing. They don't have to act full out, but they have to understand the motivations of what they're doing. A musical is rehearsed in such a disjointed fashion, because you have the musical numbers and the scenes, and you jump around. This gives them a sense of continuity and how to build the performance."

Laurents sees the difference between directing a new musical and a revival as vast. When approaching a revival he feels no obligation to attempt a reproduction of the original. On the contrary, "I think it's a mistake to do a revival as a duplication of the original. I'm not talking about regional theatres," which he believes are obliged to do reproductions due to financial and audience considerations. For himself, however, "if I didn't have a new take on it, I wouldn't do it." Referring to his 1974 revival of *Gypsy*: "What I did with Angie was very different from what [Ethel] Merman did [in the original 1959 production]. There was a problem with that show that I didn't figure out till I directed it with Angela Lansbury in London, which was at the end of 'Rose's Turn' Ethel Merman stopped and took a bow. It was awful. She stepped right out [of character] and just bowed." In London with Lansbury, Laurents found a way to keep Merman's bow, while at the same time making it work for the show. "The whole number is in her head. So, when she bows," she is bowing to the imaginary audience "in her head. The way I made that clear was the lights began to go out, the spotlight goes out on her, and she keeps bowing. The audience is no longer applauding, and they realize to their horror that this woman is loony-tunes. It was a big risk for Angie to take the first time we tried it, because if it didn't work it would just seem as though she was milking the bow. But she was wonderful, and it worked."

His revival with Tyne Daly fifteen years later was an even greater departure from the original. "What I did with Tyne was *much* different, and finally close to what I really wanted it to be. Because I thought it was very sexual; that Rose and Herbie really have a hot relationship. That's what kept it going. Otherwise, why are they together? She's walking all over him. There must be something. Also, Rose is common as dirt. She's really common and vulgar. You could do that with Tyne. That was exciting to do because you were doing the show very differently."

Laurents finds kids very easy to direct, having worked with them in both of his *Gypsy* revivals. "Don't give them, 'Count two, then smile, then turn, then go like that.'" Rather, he suggests, the key is to treat them as one would any other actor. "Tell them what they're doing. They understand. They can do anything." If overly directed, he warns, then a show can end up with "manufactured children" on stage. "The thing is, they're kids! Kids enjoy themselves—let them alone. One of them is going to be a big show-off; that's the one that plays Baby June. She's hideous, and let her be hideous." He finds children around eight years of age to be ideal for the stage, for they are old enough to reason without being too self-conscious. There are some exceptions to that rule, and he points to Brett Tabisel, who played Billy in the original Broadway production of *Big* (1996), as an example of a "really good" adolescent actor. The other children on stage in that production, however, "were so phoney . . . I really wanted to machine-gun them down."

Laurents believes out-of-town tryouts are "absolutely essential" to the success of a musical, "but it's rare because it's expensive." Furthermore, he notes, any out-of-town tryout must be budgeted long enough to serve its purpose. With *Anyone Can Whistle*, for example, "We were only out of town for ten days which was very destructive"; it was just time enough to recognize the show's faults without enough time to solve them. He does not, however, believe starting a musical's Broadway quest in the regional theatre system as a viable alternative to out-of-town tryouts. He sees two problems with this. The first is attracting quality talent ("you can't get good people to go there"); the second is "the taste is different. What looks good in Poughkeepsie suddenly is a disaster [in New York City]." Nor does he think of previewing on Broadway as an option. "It's terrible to have to pull a show together—a new, untried show—in New York." He believes *Nick and Nora*, which lasted a mere week after officially opening on Broadway, would have had a longer life if it had been afforded an out-of-town tryout, rather than opening cold in New York; for among other reasons, it would have been able to avoid a lot of the negative gossip that circulated around the city. "The *New York Times* killed me every Friday [in the gossip column] and the other papers did it on Tuesday and Wednesday. That show was dead in the water before it opened. The *New York Times* review began, 'Well, it isn't as bad as you've heard.' That's reviewing gossip," a practice Laurents sees as detrimental to the theatre; a show should be judged on its merits alone, and not on whether its road to opening was smooth or rocky, or how many changes it went through.

Though a writer on some projects and a director on others, he believes it is the director's, not the writer's, responsibility to keep the play in shape after opening. "Unlike a lot of [other directors], I go back regularly and give notes to the whole cast." He never stays away from a show long enough for it to develop into something other than the creative team's original production. Along with giving notes, "I talk to them about acting. It keeps them fresh and interested. They love it." With reminders such as "The enemy of 'excellence' is 'good,'" he continues throughout a show's run to encourage quality performances.

After decades of work and success in the musical theatre, Laurents is often asked to sit in on developing shows and offer his advice and criticisms. He admits that he accepts these invitations far less frequently than he did earlier in is career. Known for being very outspoken, he finds, "When people ask you what you think, they don't really want to know. I say to them up front, 'If you really want an opinion, I will give it to you. Otherwise, don't ask.'" At the same time, Laurents likes to see good shows succeed, and if he can offer a comment or suggestion that benefits its development, then he does. "It all depends *when*. You can't go two nights before it opens and give them an opinion. It's too late. But if it's a friend, and it's early, then I say what I think, if I think it will help. I don't think friends help by saying, 'Oh, it's wonderful. Don't change anything.'"

There are a number of aspects to Laurents's directorial philosophy that he finds vital to being a successful director of musicals. The first in importance, which he believes other directors often put last, is experience working with actors. "Every dancer in the chorus must be considered an actor. You're creating a world up there, and every dancer and singer, no matter how small his part, is a part of that world." Next he feels the director must be somebody who knows how to work with other creative artists. "There is a tendency for the directors of musicals to be very autocratic. I say that the director is the captain of the ship. His word is last, but let the other people have their word." Directors must be secure enough with themselves and their talent to trust other people. "What I have found is that people who are secure ask for help. The people who aren't say, 'Get out!' They're afraid of being questioned because they don't know the answers. It's no crime not to have the answers. Maybe someone else will come up with one." Common sense, "a sensible ego," and strength of character are also necessary traits. "A musical is a tremendous responsibility. You have to be very strong. No matter if you're quaking inside. And nobody can see it. Because it's an enormous enterprise and you have to run it." Furthermore, he suggests, "It's very helpful if you can think fast on your feet, because you have to in a musical." Although success has brought him celebrity status over the years, it is the work that Laurents cherishes above all else: "My joy comes from the doing, and anything after that is gravy."

Richard Maltby Jr.

Richard Maltby has a unique foothold in the musical theatre, working as both a director and lyricist. He has supplied lyrics to David Shire's music for a number of revues and musicals, among them *Starting Here, Starting Now* (1977), *Baby* (1984), *Closer Than Ever* (1989), and *Big* (1996), worked as co-lyricist with Alain Boublil for *Miss Saigon* (1991), and provided the lyrics for *Nick and Nora* (1991). In addition to directing most of the Maltby/Shire shows (*Starting Here, Starting Now*; *Baby*; and *Closer Than Ever* [co-directed with Steven Scott Smith]),

All quotes are taken from personal interviews conducted by the author with Mr. Maltby.

he has also directed Andrew Lloyd Webber's *Song and Dance* (1984; which he adapted for Broadway), *Fosse* (1999; co-directed with Ann Reinking), and the Fats Waller musical revue *Ain't Misbehavin'* (1978) for which he received a Tony Award.

For Maltby, directing a musical "is so different from directing a play that they should have a different word for it. It seems to use the same elements, it seems to use the same skills, but in fact the way you apply the skills is so completely different that the things you know about directing a play are virtually not applicable." Maltby comes to directing with an instinctive understanding of the craft. "I think I was fundamentally a director—I think that was my impulse. I only became a writer because I wanted to put the shows on the stage and someone had to write them." Having been "just the lyricist on a bunch of shows" and unhappy "seeing the material not come off well" by other directors, Maltby, at the age of thirty, decided to take charge of his own productions. "I thought, 'How bad could I be? Could I be any worse than anybody who ever directed anything of mine?' And the answer was 'no.' So then I was freed to do it."

Around the time he began directing, Maltby decided to take an acting class to better acquaint himself with the actor's task. The class culminated in him being cast in a two-character play. "It was a totally eye-opening experience for me. I had never understood several things that actors had told me. I didn't understand how alive you are on the stage; how you can deal with four or five things at the same time, with all the obligations of the scene plus the audience plus everything else. You're aware of the lights and the backstage, and at the same time completely focused on what you're doing. Like in a war, your mind operates on three or four levels—more than it usually does during an ordinary day." When his director incorporated a number of changes and rewrites, Maltby was thrown. "I realized that what I had done with the play in the course of rehearsing it was construct a structure for the whole thing. And because of that, it wasn't just a problem of adding this [particular change or rewrite], but it affected *everything*! You had to basically rethink the dynamic of everything else you were doing." This acting experience has proved immensely helpful to Maltby as a director when giving his own actors changes. "Writers and directors think, 'Just give them the scene, put it in, and they'll go learn it.' But what an actor does is take a relatively limited number of moments and link them together in some way so that [they] can construct a character. If you alter that—take away this line and give it to someone else, or add four lines (explaining something that they have been carefully working out how to do *without* it being explained)—it's a large adjustment."

With few exceptions, Maltby has always had a hand in writing the shows he has directed. Although, even if only serving as lyricist on a production, he believes the director, and not the writers, should serve as the final editor of the script and score. Working as both writer and director, he believes, makes his work as a director easier, and he does not have difficulty separating the two jobs: "There's sort of an auteur aspect to a director in any musical. They really control the overall design and structure of the show. And since that's what you're working on, it's not really a terribly difficult task to then go home and write a portion of it." He admits that the collaborators (including the director) often cross lines during the writing process: "It's difficult because you don't want to step on people's toes, but very often structure *is* writing." He notes that a good director is not merely the leader of the collaborators but also a contributing artist: "It's not surprising that people who understand the nature of musicals, like Hal Prince, have had numerous successful musicals, because they understand the inner life of it. And they tend to be more than simply captains of the ship, they actually are creators of the ship."

For Maltby, "the directing of a musical is an authorship function. Because I'm a director-writer, I'm always partially thinking as a writer."

For this reason, he likes to be brought on board at the inception of a project when he can still be influential in the show's development. If given the choice, he prefers directing his own work for it allows him a freedom to contribute and adapt the material throughout the process, not always the case when working with someone else's material. "I directed a staged reading of a musical version of [the film] *Arthur*, for which I didn't write anything. I thought my work on it was relatively perfunctory. I basically did what they wrote. Oh, I asked for some structural things to focus the action up a little bit which they went off and did. But I didn't find it a particularly exciting experience." Early in his career Maltby dabbled with directing plays, including productions of *Long Day's Journey into Night* and *The Glass Menagerie*, but found little enjoyment in it. "I couldn't understand directing without adjusting. The idea of just directing *The Glass Menagerie* because that's the way it is bothered me. Because I'm accustomed to the sort of on-your-feet creativity [in] shaping the shows."

Maltby would not recommend that other director-writers mount their own works unless they can—as he does—separate the two jobs entirely. "I can only do it because I'm completely schizophrenic in it. When I'm standing there with the actors and directing it, I have no memory of writing it. I am quite capable of looking at a line that I wrote in a song and saying, 'Well now, why did the author write this instead of that?' and talk as if I've never seen it before. Because, literally, I don't remember writing it." He also has no proprietary interest in his own writing: "I'm not tied to what I wrote [and] I'm not protective of it." He believes this allows his actors a freedom to take the material off the page and breathe new life into it. "An actor dealing with a song or a scene is completely different from the author dealing with a scene, and I'm very willing to let a song turn into something I didn't expect once the actors start dealing with it." He believes, "If you can separate yourself as George Abbott was able to do, or [George S.] Kaufman was able to do, or think of the whole thing as some sort of elaborate writing assignment and that what you get the actors to do is some *version* of what you're writing, then you can do it. [But] if you are a controlling author who wants to have it the way he wrote it, then the actors will feel very nervous because they won't have anybody to turn to. They can't say to the person who wrote the scene, 'I don't understand this, it just doesn't make any sense to me.' That's what directors are for." The director must serve as the liaison. He can then either help the actor to better understand the scene or go back to the writer for clarification and possible rewrites. Either way, the two jobs must be separated. "If there's too much ego involved in the writing process or the directing process, then you can't do it."

Maltby believes he, as well as most every other director in the American musical theatre, has been directly or indirectly influenced by the work of three great directors. "Take away Jerry Robbins, Hal Prince, and George Abbott and what musical theatre do you have left? They *are* musical theatre. They are the people who learned all the lessons, and theirs are the shows that sit up there and tell you how to do it." The one common denominator among them all is their understanding of structure. "The great directing artists—the greatest, I think, being Jerome Robbins—were all about structure. *Gypsy* [1959], *West Side Story* [1957], and *Fiddler on the Roof* [1964] are just brilliantly structured." This has had a tremendous influence on Maltby's own career. "Structure is everything"; it should consume the director "from the time you say, 'I'm going to direct this,' to the time you open. You could spend endless hours coaching a scene," only to find that "what matters is not at all the coaching of the scene, what matters is how that scene is fitting into the flow of the whole show. The design of the whole show takes precedence over everything, and everything becomes a function of the design of the whole piece. The shows that don't succeed usually have a tremendous flabbiness in their storytelling."

Maltby learned structure from a number of different sources, the first being his father, a music arranger and orchestrator: "Within a two-and-a-half minute arrangement of a song everything had a kind of perfect clockwork to it: this happened, then this happened, and it all came together and ended. I got that from listening to [my father's] arrangements." He also learned another form of structure through his work directing musical revues, that of "running orders." "Suddenly it just became clear that if you do an opening number and then some introductory remarks, the next [number] had better be really high. And then you don't go immediately down, you stay pretty high on the [third] one. If you've got a nodder in there somewhere you can do it in the fourth spot." These fundamental dynamics of a score do not merely apply to musical revues but to book musicals as well: "Musicals are stories and they are also revues. In a show like *My Fair Lady* [1956], even if you weren't following the story, you would have a satisfactory pattern of ballads, production numbers, comedy songs. . . . That element of a show is as important as all the other elements of the show—the sort of running order of the score."

Maltby is also a strong believer in the power of comedy in the musical theatre. "Comedy conceals structure. Everything you need to lead the audience by the nose from one end of the show to the other can be made palatable if it's done through comedy, so they don't realize they're being given naked structure." He is convinced that the first joke is the most important element of the entire show. "If it's the right one it tells you the entire evening. The definitive one being the one at the beginning of *Fiddler on the Roof.* [Tevya:] 'And we wear these little prayer shawls. Why do we wear them? I'll tell you. I don't know. But it's a tradition!' The entire plot of the show is in that joke. And suddenly the audience knows all the terms of the evening. [At the beginning of a show] the audience doesn't know anything. The show has to tell them. You can tell them boldly or you can find just exactly the right joke."

He points to the best comedy songs as being excellent examples of structure. "The classic one is 'Adelaide's Lament' [from *Guys and Dolls*; 1950], which is a total exposition song. Leaving aside the fact that it is screamingly funny, you don't know Adelaide until that song. If you took it out of the show you wouldn't know Adelaide at all. This [song] is what makes you love her, makes you interested in her. It tells you all of the back story, it tells you the plot of her trying to get married, it tells you everything. It's almost by accident that it's funny. So, the term 'comedy song' is a misleading one, because 'Adelaide's Lament' is completely there for structure." For Maltby, even the most exhilarating showstopper is a by-product of structure. "The Rain in Spain" from Lerner and Loewe's *My Fair Lady* "stops the show! It has no lyric content, no melodic content, no anything. It's just a completely exuberant coming together of all the plotlines that makes you thrill. It's structure. It's all structure."

During pre-production "the most important thing to do is define what the story is and how you're going to tell it to the audience—how you're going to command their attention." He begins by capsulizing the meaning of the show into a single sentence, a goal easily accomplished for the musical *Baby*. Although incorporating some "extraordinarily complex issues, [*Baby*] is about how the child changes the relationship. That's what the show is really all about." By reducing the essence of the show into a single sentence, he remains focused on the larger story being told and avoids getting caught up in secondary issues. In contrast to his experience with *Baby*, he says the reason he chose not to direct his musical *Big* (directed on Broadway by Mike Ockrent) was because "I didn't feel that I had enough of a handle on it as a director. I felt that somebody else should come in and shape it. And I think that's probably why it failed. Not because someone else came in, but because when all is said and done, it hadn't shaken down to a sentence, to a single thing I could hold onto." Once the director has defined the show, he or she must then be careful to avoid incorporating "all the things that just seem nice, because that's what we do in musicals. Musicals use artificial means to get to truth—singing, dancing, comedy, costumes, everything. But there is inherent in all that stuff an emotional basis, which sometimes gets obscured in the mere stylistic elements of musicals. The trick is to somehow cut through it and find where the heart is beating underneath. There's nothing wrong with the glitz of the musical theatre if it serves what you're doing, but make sure it really does what it says it's going to do. Don't think that it [alone] is inherently interesting."

Once a show's "essence" has been discerned, a set must be designed to support it. Maltby assumes the task of being the editor of the design elements: "Throwing out is one of the major skills of a director." Interestingly, for someone who started out with aspirations of being a set designer, as Maltby did, he finds now that as a director he wants very little scenery. "I seem to be a minimalist. The shows that I've written [and directed] have no real need for a lot of physical production." This may hold true for his work as a director, but not for the shows he has written, *Miss Saigon* (directed by Nicholas Hytner) being the obvious exception. However, Maltby believes *Miss Saigon* could be reproduced in a less elaborate form: "That show could be done much, much simpler [because it] is largely a bunch of two- and three-character scenes." He foresees future productions taking this path. Maltby wields a considerable understanding of scenic design, which aids his ability to collaborate with designers. "A really good set ought to completely work *for* you. Sometimes, if you haven't really thought it through, if you haven't really dealt with the set as a function of the story, you get it on stage and the set has a life of its own, and you begin altering the show to justify the set." If he had his choice he would much prefer the opportunity to rehearse and stage a show prior to designing the set, as he and designer Robin Wagner were able to do while developing *Song and Dance* in a workshop prior to opening on Broadway. This allowed the set to be tailored to the demands of the script and the characters. But, he admits, that style of collaboration proves impractical when mounting most Broadway productions. In general, he is much more interested in developing and presenting three-dimensional characters than three-dimensional settings. His belief is that audiences, for the most part, do not need to know most of the information an overblown set bombards upon them. "You don't need to know in mundane settings where the walls are in the room. You don't need to know where the doors are. You don't need extra props or tables." What you *do* need to know are the characters. Characters are the essence.

Maltby believes "casting is just about everything. Almost any director will tell you that 80 percent of the job is casting." As half of a songwriting team, it is not surprising that he is "usually looking for singers who can act. To do David's [Shire] and my stuff you've got to really sing. You've got to hit those high notes. You've got to have control. Anything that we do requires a certain kind of singing skill to begin with, and then a kind of acting skill on top of that." This is his approach in casting book musicals as well as revues. In an audition, a strong singer who "plays a kind of scene" is what catches his attention. "If they [the performer] have a lot of skill in singing but it doesn't seem connected to anything, that doesn't interest me much." Maltby feels the tide has turned in terms of acting style in the musical theatre. "Years ago when we were doing *Starting Here, Starting Now* I really had to train singers to act. There was a much bigger musical comedy vocabulary and these sorts of acting-operetta parts had not come along. So, I really had to say a lot of, 'No, no, don't sell it. Don't embellish it. Just tell me the story. Just tell me the truth.' I almost never have to say that now because there's a whole crop of singing actors we've developed. What there *isn't* is flash. What there isn't is a whole crop of singer-dancers who know how to sell a number." He admits one of the problems of casting

Fosse, a retrospective of Bob Fosse's choreography from the 1950s to the 1980s, was "finding dancers who [could] sing and be sort of vaude-villians too"; the young performers, Maltby discovered, were embarrassed to be performing in such a broad, musical comedy style of an earlier era.

He has few hard-and-fast rules on how he matches the characters on the page with the right actor or actress in an audition. "I have discovered that every time I have tried to cast carefully for the obligations of the part, nothing happens." Nowadays, he is much more apt to cast someone based on their innate talent as a performer than on qualities they may share with the character. His impulse is to cast "wildly talented" people "and then make the part serve the talents of that person. That's the big impulse of casting a star. If you know somebody is terrifically talented and kind of right for the part, then that *becomes* right for the part." This is exemplified in Maltby's casting of Bernadette Peters in *Song and Dance* and then molding the show around her abilities. Because *Song and Dance* is, in essence, a one-woman show, the need for casting a "star" became important, and Maltby recognizes their place in the musical theatre. "Musicals are a bastardized form and are about entertainment. You have to deliver thrills at regular intervals. Stars give a kind of electricity; they are stars because they *have* this electricity. And that becomes inherently interesting."

Sometimes it works in the opposite direction: instead of casting stars, *Ain't Misbehavin'* made stars. Maltby admits he began auditions for that revue "not knowing what the show was going to be" and looking initially for only three performers, not the five into which it eventually developed. "Armelia McQueen came in and I thought, 'She is so exotic and extraordinary. I've got to have her.' Then an hour later Nell [Carter] came in. 'That voice! I've got to have her.' And then Irene Cara came in." Maltby found himself with three women and two men (Andre De Shields and Ken Page), all of whom he wanted to cast. It was during this change of direction in the casting process (from three characters to five) that the through-line of the show developed. "I thought, 'Great! One of the women is without a man, and if she wants a man she's going to have to break up a couple. I have tension going here!' And, in fact, that's what the whole play is about: relationships that last and don't last. The end of the first act [for example] is nothing but fast recouplings as everybody splits around." Here again Maltby condensed the essence of the show into a single sentence and shaped the production around the performers he cast.

His rehearsal schedule can change according to the demands of the individual production. "The shows I've done have been so different. With *Ain't Misbehavin'* we went in with a pile of music, a bunch of ideas, and a gleam in our eye; it was arranged and everything was sort of done in rehearsal. *Song and Dance* is basically a one-woman show [and] it had already been produced in England. Some of the other shows that I've done a more standard rehearsal period on, I've never felt very good about. I didn't feel that a spark ever happened with those shows." Some rehearsal schedules, however, are forced to change due to unforeseen circumstances. For example, "We threw out the entire second act of *Baby* on the first day of rehearsal."

Once in rehearsal, he prefers to take time to examine the script and characters with the cast before attempting to stage it. "I like to read the script a lot before it gets on its feet." With *Song and Dance*, "we sat at the table for almost two weeks just defining the character [before] I finally said, 'I think we better block it.'" Rehearsals for *Baby*, due to the early elimination of the second act, were a bit less structured. "*Baby* was involved in so much revision. We improvised, we played, if we had a new scene we played with it, rewrote it the next day."

Occasionally, Maltby will incorporate theatre games into his rehearsal process if he feels, as he did with *Baby*, that "the specifics of the characters were completely flexible." By the time *Baby* began formal rehearsals, many of the cast members were familiar with the material having presented it numerous times in backer's auditions and a workshop production. However, "I wanted them to know their characters separate from the play. So, before they went into rehearsal on the first day, I gave them an assignment to fill up ten minutes of stage time any way they wanted. They could do an improvisation, they could do it with dialogue [from the script], they could do it without dialogue, they could do a pantomime scene, it could be anything. We started the first day with a reading of the script and the discovery that the second act was in real trouble. Then we did these [assignments]." Through these exercises intended to expand the actors' understanding of their characters, Maltby was enlightened by the company's grasp of the show's central theme. "These turned out to be the key to the rewrite of the show." The musical, in trouble just hours earlier, was now on the road to recovery, all from a spontaneous acting exercise.

Once he has gotten the show on its feet, he often discovers unexpected and necessary alterations. "If you're dealing with clever writers who have already done their job, you may find that you can put the opening on stage just exactly the way it is [written]." Although he notes, "In many cases, there's something off about it," which needs to be adjusted by the director. In the case of "the helicopter scene" ("The Fall of Saigon") from *Miss Saigon,* the director, Nicholas Hytner, did not have to alter the author's work at all. According to Maltby, the scene was first laid out musically (to insure the number's build), then the lyrics and scenes were applied. "Nick listened to that [and] worked out with the set designer [John Napier] how to do it. The director did not shape it. He staged exactly what [we had] written. That's very unusual. It's usually altered." In *Miss Saigon's* case, "[as] in the opera tradition, when you have an exciting piece of music you figure out what to do with it, you don't try and alter it."

He does not pre- or paper block his shows ahead of time, because he feels this limits the cast's creativity. "I find that anytime I have an idea in my head before I go in, all I do is straightjacket everybody." He admits that for elaborate scenes "where traffic is a major issue," he will sometimes work out patterns ahead of time. But, in general, his approach to creating movement on stage is to focus on the actors first. "I try to see what they [the actors] instinctively want to do, and then just pull from that, occasionally go a little further with that, occasionally take something out. But I want it to come instinctively." He seeks movement that is not only instinctive to the character but also to the actor, so that it becomes a natural extension of both. For Maltby, the actor is at the core of every character, and one cannot make demands on a character that the actor cannot fulfill. Most small scenes and songs, he admits he does not formally block at all, but instead prefers to let the actors work out the details in response to the needs of the script.

When staging musical numbers, "I'm very much of the 'stand-still-and-don't-move-unless-you-need-to-move' school. There's a song called 'Crossword Puzzle' [in *Starting Here, Starting Now*] which Loni Ackerman did and I never staged that. She just did it over and over again. It slowly set itself." He prefers to give his actors the parameters of the scene and the tools necessary to express it properly, then allow them to interpret it within that context. From that evolves the blocking for the scene. "Everything is accomplished in the preparation. That is to say, in the minute before you [the actor] go on, or the minute before you start to sing. You have to be in the right emotional place. I almost never stage a ballad or anything like that. I just try to get them in the right place before the song starts and then see what their instinct is." From that point he allows his actors to "release it and let the song go wherever it goes." The blocking then "usually happens naturally." For example, "Ken Page was doing 'Your Feet's Too Big' [from *Ain't Misbehavin'*]. The song was always done as an entertainment song. I did it as a scene." Maltby established Page's character sitting at a table in a bar, holding a glass, and just drunk enough to let out the unspeakable thought. He told Page his companion had just gone to the ladies' room, "'and because she's gone you can let it all out!' I gave him those specifics, he sang it once, and I said, 'Freeze that.' He just did it instinctively. Now, we changed a few details to stand up here and give it a climax there," but for all intent and purposes, the scene that Maltby established and Ken Page interpreted was set. "Set the terms, then let it happen. And then what happens will usually be right."

Maltby admits, "I don't altogether trust choreographers. They often impose something on the moment. Because that's what choreography sort of is, taking it and imposing a movement style on an emotion. You have to be very careful that what [the actors] are *doing* doesn't communicate something that is against, or get in the way of, what they're *saying*." For this reason, he likes to either stage his own musical numbers himself if he can, or work side by side with the choreographer to achieve the right look and style for a number. With *Ain't Misbehavin'*, Maltby first blocked a lot of the numbers himself, then brought in choreographer Arthur Faria to build off of his original ideas. Maltby prefers choreography that adds to and heightens a musical moment, as opposed to dance for the sake of dance, and he points to Jerome Robbins as a craftsman with the perfect balance: "Jerry Robbins did it so that you absolutely understood the scene that was playing underneath it."

What he appreciates most from choreography is the sense of "style" it brings to the musical theatre. "It's not surprising that choreographers have become directors of musicals because they give it a stylistic quality from the very beginning. The trouble is that they're often not literary, and therefore have trouble organizing a story that requires literary organization." Maltby found himself in such a dilemma with *Song and Dance*. "I thought there was a way the second act ballet could relate to the first act [one-woman opera], and I wrote an outline for that. The trouble was I wasn't the choreographer, so I was at the mercy of the dramatization of Peter Martins [choreographer], who is not a theatre person. I loved working with him. I thought he did a beautiful job. But it wasn't truthful enough. It didn't depict a real New York that I thought it could have."

Maltby has found particular success with musical revues. When he first began directing he staged a number of nightclub acts. That experience, along with his years mounting the Manhattan Theatre Club benefit revues, has given him a great deal of practical exposure to the form. Ironically, he admits: "I don't like revues. I don't think a revue is inherently very delightful." Because of that he always tries to make more out of a revue than just a progression of musical numbers strung together. "I give revues a lot of structure. A series of things that are just sort of nice in a row doesn't interest me. So, I push to make them link in some other kind of way." For instance, "a show like *Ain't Misbehavin'* is linked on all sorts of levels, other than its being a revue. It's an anomaly, because you can't call it anything but a revue since it's just one number [after another]. Except revues don't have characters, and *Ain't Misbehavin'* has characters . . . they don't have plots or lives, but they have forward motion, and you keep seeing them. And because it's intended to dramatize Fats Waller, it has biographical material [giving it a] sense of period, a sense of time. All of that was put in the show by design. Which is why it's so rich. It's pure structure." It is not surprising then that he sees very little difference between directing a revue and directing a book musical.

Overall, Maltby believes the director must remain focused throughout the rehearsal process by continuing to "dig through and ask: What is the truth? What is the surprise? What is going to startle your audience?" He is not necessarily referring to big surprises; subtle surprises can, at times, be just as effective: "[Surprise] can come from the unexpected illumination of the human heart." These surprises are tools the writer gives the director to help keep the audience interested. "A show has exactly the same impulses as a storyteller. If I want to tell you an anecdote, I set it up, I lead you there. If I have to tell you a back story before I get to the story, I make sure I let you know. Then I go. Those devices are not different on the stage, and any number of things can do that to make sure that you listen. Mystery can do it, suspense can do it, leaving out essential pieces of information that you're going to give them later on can do it. There's an arsenal of things that can do it." Once a director stops asking these questions and allows himself to be satisfied, the development of the story ceases. Additionally, Maltby pays particular attention to pace. The director, he says, should have "a sense of impatience—an impatience that reflects an audience's impatience. You want to be given the information and then you want to get on."

The role of the producer in the musical theatre, he believes, has a limited but vital role in the creative aspect of a show. "The creative element of producing is knowing what the fundamental story is and keeping everybody on track. At certain moments you go off track—everybody does—and that's the moment the producer ought to come in and say, 'You said we were going to feel this. I'll tell you, the scene comes and I don't feel *any*thing.' Or, 'You said it was about this, and there are all these scenes with this other character. I'm not getting the story.'" He also points out that while a producer can be a great arbitrator for "squabbles" among the creative team, there is a right and a wrong way to keep the collaborators moving in the proper direction: "Not [by saying], 'you're right and you're wrong,' but 'the show was going to be this, and it seems to me this is where it has to go.' Now, if you're bright enough to do that, you're probably bright enough to be a bad director."

Maltby likes to check back on a show once it has opened to insure a high-quality production. "Maybe because I'm a writer *and* director, I go back all the time." Keeping a show consistent can be challenging.

When a show does begin to change, Maltby steps in and corrects the problem, as he did during the run of *Ain't Misbehavin'*. "The Broadway production kept speeding up. It got so fast it was breakneck. You couldn't hear any of the words any more. Some of the jokes didn't land [because] you just didn't hear them." Eventually he was able to slow the pace of the show to its original Broadway opening tempo. Ironically, once that restoration was accomplished, the actors found it difficult to perform: "The actors would come off stage feeling like they had been dragging this enormous weight because they didn't know how to play it that slow [any longer]." He prefers to rehearse cast replacements himself, but he will sometimes turn whole shows over to another member of the production for governing and remountings. "I finally got to the point with *Ain't Misbehavin'* where I let Arthur Faria do the production because he does it superbly, better than I could do. It's a dance piece really—a piece of dance-theatre—[and] he knows where every pinky goes. I actually can't direct a production of *Ain't Misbehavin'* anymore because it's so choreographed."

He views New York as the true test for any musical. "New York is a tough place, but on a certain level I'm glad it is. I didn't like being on the receiving end of its calumny [with *Big*], but it does stand for something—some higher level of work." During *Big*, Maltby felt out of place on Broadway for the first time in his career. "I was walking down the street to the Shubert Theatre one day—I guess we were starting techs—and I just had the sense that we weren't welcome. I've never been able to understand the venom that was attached to *Big*. There was a huge number of people who thought *Big* was the anti-Christ!" Although New York is the proving ground, Maltby has often used the regional theatre system (most notably the Williamstown Theatre Festival in Massachusetts) to workshop projects before bringing them into the city. This allows him a creative freedom without the commitment or pressure of an impending New York production, a pressure inherent in an out-of-town tryout leading directly to Broadway.

Because he is primarily a self-taught director who has been influenced by a variety of different sources, Maltby is unsure where young directors can best learn the craft. He does not dismiss university training programs as being a possible feeder system for the professional theatre, but he does not believe they properly prepare up-and-coming directors to further, rather than merely recycle, the musical theatre through the development of original works. "Doing productions of *The Music Man* is one thing, it's a skill, and making it come alive takes a lot of doing. But it just isn't the same as being given a script and a bunch of songs and trying to make the show come together."

Maltby feels that, above all else, the director of a musical must "define the structure" of the work being presented. "The structure might have already been defined by the author, and all you [have to do] is understand what their structure is and make it happen—if you're lucky. In most cases, [however,] musicals are too complicated. This process makes it sound sort of easy, but it leads to disasters" if not handled correctly. A good director has both a broad base of knowledge and an in-depth theatrical understanding: "You have to know storytelling. You have to know and enjoy the trappings of musical theatre. You have to understand what choreography means, what dancing is, what staging is, what shtick is, what sight gags are, and all of that. And yet not be fooled by them, and not think they are inherently interesting. You have to know how to thrill an audience. That doesn't mean skyrockets going off or the helicopter coming in [from *Miss Saigon*], and it doesn't necessarily mean *good* news. Thrilling is the last moment in *Long Day's Journey into Night* when you see the family together and you totally understand the madness. It's tragic, it's horrifying, but it's thrilling.

"A lot of directing as far as I'm concerned is setting up things so they can happen. Setting up talented people to do their best work. Setting up a show" so it can "explode" with delight for an audience. "We're in the business of astonishing. Astonishing things are loud voices, incredible talent, beautiful things to look at, costume parades like the black-and-white Ascot scene in *My Fair Lady*, just pure melody like 'Bess, You Is My Woman Now' [from *Porgy and Bess*; 1935], two voices hitting high notes, emotional feeling, emotional realities, discoveries about the passion of the human heart. You have to understand all of the miracles that can take place which you have to set in motion. An awful lot of it is asking questions. An awful lot of it is trusting what the answer is."

Des McAnuff

Canadian-born Des McAnuff moved to the United States just prior to his twenty-fourth birthday, already an established playwright, composer, and director in Toronto. He landed in New York where he became involved with the Chelsea Theatre Center, later splintering off with a group that would eventually become Dodger Productions, a major producing organization. In 1983 he took the reins as artistic director of the La Jolla Playhouse in Southern California where he worked until 1994. While there, McAnuff produced and directed a number of

All quotes are taken from personal interviews conducted by the author with Mr. McAnuff.

musicals including three that eventually made their way to Broadway: *Big River* (1985; Tony Award), *The Who's Tommy* (1993; Tony Award), and the Matthew Broderick revival of *How to Succeed in Business Without Really Trying* (1995).

One of his earliest musical theatre influences came when he was still in high school: *Hair* (1968; directed by Tom O'Horgan) spoke to McAnuff and his rock 'n' roll generation. He would eventually audition for the Toronto company and for O'Horgan himself. Although he was not selected for "the Mississauga tribe," the experience gave him the confidence to begin writing and composing his own projects for the theatre. He involved himself in every facet of play production in high school, from writing and composing to acting and directing. Once in college, he developed a broader interest in theatre beyond just the musical form. "I also found that rock 'n' roll, if you like, had more of an influence in serious drama than it did in musical theatre. Musical theatre was really developing from that kind of '50s tradition. There are exceptional geniuses like Sondheim, but for the most part, it's a different kind of music than the music that interested me, and for the most part still interests me." During his college years, he put aside his other interests (including directing) in favor of playwriting. Here he received invaluable hands-on tutorials in the professional Canadian theatre, by working with a number of professional directors on various productions of his plays. "That really was my education," he claims. Following that period, he returned to directing with renewed insight.

Both Michael Bennett and Bob Fosse indirectly influenced McAnuff's understanding of the musical. "I didn't get to know either of them directly, but I've worked with a lot of people that worked with both of them, and I daresay they've been an influence through those other people." Other influences include producer Joseph Papp, Michael Langham of the Stratford Festival in Ontario, and the Canadian director John Hirsch. Not only did these individuals pass along valuable knowledge, they also gave McAnuff important support for his work.

Although he is an advocate of educational theatre as a training ground for professional artists (having worked closely with the graduate program at U.C. San Diego while at La Jolla), he believes the director learns primarily through practical experience. "Theoretical knowledge is a wonderful thing, and it's important to acquire as much of it as possible, but when push comes to shove, you have to get into the trenches yourself and do the work." New directors must also develop their own unique voice: "You can't go see a great Bob Fosse production, and then just ape it and expect it to achieve much. You have to find your own way." Ultimately, he sees the director's best education coming from the artist's peers and contemporaries. "They're going to be your harshest critics, and probably your most effective teachers. You learn from each other, and you learn on the job." Therein lies the catch, according to McAnuff: How does the director get the directing job? "If you're an actor, you can get hired. If you're a director, you generally have to initiate projects." He also sees assisting other directors as a worthwhile path into the professional theatre. Michael Greif, for example, director of the Broadway musical *Rent* (1996) and successor to McAnuff as artistic director of the La Jolla Playhouse, "was first my student at La Jolla, and then my assistant."

"It's hard to imagine anything much more complicated than tackling a new musical. It is a huge undertaking. They sweep you along like a tidal wave, and you can do nothing but, once you're in the middle of one. That is your life, when you're directing a musical." For this reason he chooses projects he is not only passionate about but also with which he has made a personal connection. "I'm selfishly interested in my own life and times. So, it's important to me that I can relate personally to every experience. And that has a great deal to do with passion, too. I don't think this is some abstract concept, that you take on a particular project because it happens to stir your interest. I think it generally has to do with something more selfish than that. It's something you can understand on a personal level." However, he suggests young directors should not limit their opportunities to learn the craft and skills needed to mount musicals; practical experience is at times more important than passion for the material.

McAnuff refers to himself as "an eclectic director" who has "probably done more Shakespeare and Chekhov" than he has musicals. After directing a musical he is apt to change gears entirely and direct a different form of theatre. "I don't think I could direct musicals exclusively. If I've [just] done a new musical then my impulse is probably going to be to do a new play [next], or to do *A Midsummer Night's Dream*, or perhaps to do a classic musical. I'm much more interested in content than style." He believes his experience directing classical works makes him a better director of musicals than he would be otherwise. "There are a couple basic groups of directors: there are directors who come at the musical from within the musical—they're dancers who become choreographers who become directors, or they're producers who become directors—and that has its own tradition and its own set of principles and values and approaches. And then you get another school, and they approach the musical quite differently, in that they tend to come, like I do, from drama. And you bring those aesthetics and approaches and principles."

McAnuff believes that performance is a principle area of the director's charge and that directors should have performance experience if they are to inspire great work from their actors. "It's not enough that you do great work. What's really critical is that you bring great work out of a number of other people. I think studying acting can be a great advantage." McAnuff studied acting with Vasya Hunter who "didn't just give us one system, she actually sketched a number of different approaches." He finds that education invaluable when working with performer's various approaches. "Actors have a whole host of different ways of tackling a role. I think it's folly to try to impose a particular approach on an actor. It may not apply to them at all." However, directors do not have to be great actors in order to acquire the skills that will aid them. He says, "It's often baseball managers who have been mediocre players that manage the most successful teams." He does not feel the ability to read music is a prerequisite to directing musicals. "I think it matters more for the stage manager who's having to call the show. I think that the most important thing is that you're musical. Which means that you have to have a sense of melody and harmony, and you have to be sensitive emotionally to music. But I don't think you have to be a brilliant music student to direct musicals."

He does not consciously direct a musical differently than he does a play, although he notes "there's no question it's a different beast. I think directing a musical may require more strength. I don't necessarily think it's about being dictatorial, but I do think it's about being strong. If [for example] there's some song that someone's married to and you really feel that [it] is getting in the way of the structure of an act, that's a fight you'd better win. I don't necessarily believe in creation through crisis. I've met others that believe this [but] it just doesn't seem to work that well to me. On the other hand, I've also watched people who I think are passive, and I think that's also not acceptable. You have to have a sense of where you're going. It's your job to keep the overview of the project so you don't get sidetracked, [and] end up exploring a tributary instead of carrying on down the main stream of the project." Combined with being a strong leader, he works diligently to encourage his company to be creative and offer suggestions so he can take full advantage of all the creative forces available.

McAnuff views the director's job on a musical as being a contributing collaborator along with the rest of the creative team. "If you're doing a new musical, I think with contemporary stage craft and just the way the whole genre has evolved, you are inherently involved as a creator.

You are a principal storyteller . . . and you must take that part of the job very seriously. You're just as responsible as the composer or the book writer or the lyricist. You have a large responsibility in terms of telling that story, shaping it dramaturgically, structurally, and so on. You have to be in the middle of that team." As one of the creators of the work, he sees the director as having as much as, but no more, editorial power than the writers. In general, he tries to achieve a consensus among the creative team when editing, rather than simply dictate cuts and alterations to the script and score. Sometimes, he admits, the director must orchestrate that consensus. "If you have a particular agenda for a sequence, then you need to have the persuasive powers to convince your collaborators that that's the way to go."

Although still collaborative, McAnuff wields a stronger hand when coordinating the design elements. "Over the physical production you have a lot to say. And you *need* to have a lot to say about it, because you have to sign off on every decision. But you're working with people at the pinnacle of their professions, and so you'd better also listen to what they have to say. Generally, if there's a problem and you're working with good people, you'll all eventually identify the same problem and you'll solve it as a team." For him, it is important that the director give himself plenty of time during pre-production to develop the show and its designs: "You'd better make sure you've got a good blue-sky period to dream up the production." It is only when the creative team is unhurried and unpressured (far from deadlines) that they can be truly contemplative about their work. "Once you actually start rehearsals, you really are on a treadmill, and efficiency does become important. You have a finite amount of time, and you have to use the hours really effectively." Working out the designs can happen in a number of different ways. "In some cases, I might have a very clear idea visually what I want. In other cases, [as] with *Tommy*, we started working on the design before there was a script. I could just talk [John Arnone, set designer] through the song order. We had the liner notes from the album, and I would describe the story I was telling. And the design evolved out of that kind of process."

Also critical for him during pre-production is the score. Whether working on a new musical or a revival, he spends a considerable amount of time with the creative team working out everything from staging ideas to orchestrations. "We would make a pass at pretty much every song in pre-production. The music director, the orchestrator (if they're available), my assistants, the choreographer—we would actually work through the show, sketch everything in advance in pre-production. So, we would have a pretty good handle on more or less the whole project, musically." Throughout this process, he avoids setting decisions in stone and tries to leave flexibility in the show's development, noting the influence the performers will have on the work once rehearsals begin.

"I went through a period in the early '80s—I did four or five projects in a row where I had to replace an actor. And I came to realize toward the end of this period that it was my fault. It had nothing to do with the actor. They were miscast. They weren't fulfilling something that I required, and I wasn't able to go on with them." This experience served as a wake-up call for McAnuff, making him much more cautious and judicious in his casting choices. He now spends as much time as possible with each performer during the audition to not only assess the actor's strengths, weaknesses, range, and personality but also to let them know what he expects of them, how he works, and how he is approaching the show. His efforts are intended to eliminate any possible surprises with cast members once rehearsals begin. To this end, he is apt to see actors on numerous occasions through a series of callback auditions. When casting mistakes occur, however, he recommends replacing the actor. Not replacing them would hurt the show *and* be a disservice to the actor. "You're not doing them a favor by leaving them in the part," he asserts.

When casting either a musical or a play, McAnuff puts the emphasis on acting ability. "Acting is of paramount importance. You can get fooled into thinking that a great voice will suffice in a musical, but generally, that's not the case. [Being] a great singer or a great dancer is generally not enough. It's paramount to me that everyone on stage have considerable ability as an actor." Even in a sung-through epic musical such as *Tommy*, where a strong singing voice may initially appear to suffice, McAnuff casts the actor over the singer.

One of the primary reasons for directing *How to Succeed*, says McAnuff, was the fact that Matthew Broderick was already signed on in the lead role of J. Pierpont Finch. A star's involvement in a production can be a tremendous asset, although "I think you still have to be careful not to miscast. The bottom line is great performances. That's what you really want to achieve [and] Matthew just had the right set of attributes for that part. I had a classic American clown." Sometimes a show is better served without high-profile celebrities. The creative team for *Tommy*, for example, explored the possibility of casting very well-known actors, but ultimately, "We believed that the musical itself was kind of the star, and that it was our job to cast the most capable people in those roles. Happily, Michael Cerveris came in the first day I had auditions in Los Angeles for Tommy. [It] was a very, very difficult role to cast, and I felt that he nailed it."

He prefers to vary his rehearsal techniques from show to show, tailoring them to the needs of each specific production. "I think the most satisfying journeys involve a great deal of discovery, and perhaps techniques that you may never use again, and never used before; things that pertain directly to that project." He does not have a particular style or mode of rehearsing a show, claiming: "There's some kind of chemical reaction that happens between me and the material, and it's going to influence the way I work a great deal." He admits he has gone into rehearsals at times without a completed script and score, but does not think it is a good idea unless the show is being developed specifically through the rehearsal/workshop process (as were Michael Bennett's *A Chorus Line* and George C. Wolfe's *Bring in 'da Noise/Bring in 'da Funk*). "You want to go into something where you've prepared perhaps meticulously, textually, in advance, and maybe gone through several rewrites." On rare occasions he has even begun rehearsals on plays for which he did not know the ending: "It's not necessarily the most comforting feeling."

When mounting a new musical he prefers a minimum of five weeks of rehearsal before going into the theatre, and he insists on spending the first week of that rehearsal period around the table. "I'm convinced it saves time. Not only are people going to set out on the same road stylistically but they're also going to become comfortable with each other." This time interacting as a company, and not as characters, allows the group to develop a vocabulary with one another, a process he finds critical. Moreover, this first week often affords McAnuff time to talk a bit more philosophically about the project. "When we did *A Funny Thing Happened on the Way to the Forum* [at the La Jolla Playhouse] we spent a great deal of time on Roman drama and talked about the whole evolution of the clown through history. It was a fantastic education. Now, you may only be able to afford two or three days on a big complex musical [exploring those issues], but I still think it's crucial to spend that time. I always do it on the tours, too." To aid the company in these discussions he, his assistants, and a dramaturg will do research and prepare packets of relevant material for each cast member. Principal actors and chorus alike share excerpts from the packets and explore the prepared information together. This not only educates the group but also gives each a feeling of contribution in the development of the production. During that first week McAnuff will also spend a portion of the rehearsal time teaching the company the music for the production. It is not until the second week of rehearsals that he begins staging the show.

More often than not he approaches blocking rehearsals with written staging notes—what he refers to as "a plan A." However, he is aware that during the rehearsal process, "it's often a B, C, or D plan that evolves." He is open to actors or others in the rehearsal room offering suggestions or ideas, contending, "I want the best idea in the room, wherever it comes from." Even though he realizes from the outset that his initial "plan A" will likely be augmented and improved upon by the open collaboration he extends to others, it does not stop him from being as "absolutely prepared" as possible on paper ahead of time. Such preparedness gives him and his company a foundation upon which to create and prevents wasting time during rehearsals. This written preparation can be as simple as merely noting entrances and exits or as complex as developing movement for every measure of music. "In some cases, as with *Tommy*, it required a great deal of preparation just for practical reasons. A number like 'Sparks' [a musical pantomime in which Tommy is examined by a battery of doctors and nurses] was probably five or six hours of just solid preparation with an accompanist." Otherwise "[it] would have taken two weeks to stage. There's enough staging in that one number for half an act. It was a very, very complicated sequence."

Although he is not a choreographer, he does take a hand in staging all of the musical numbers for a show, believing the director's contribution in this way makes for a more consistent production. "I call it 'sketching.' To me a musical number is about storytelling, even if it's very 'dancey.' It's not about dance really, it's about using dance as a means of telling a story. So, I really try to do the basic staging for all musical numbers." Often, he will "sketch" a number himself and then hand it over to the choreographer who takes it into the dance studio where "the moves and the blocking get transformed into 'steps.' Now, there are exceptions to this. For example, in *How to Succeed* with [the song] 'Brotherhood of Man,' Wayne [Cilento, choreographer] worked out a kind of a routine based on this notion of guys in suits dancing, this very contained movement gradually busting out. So, in that situation, I was applying what he had done in advance." At other times, he and the choreographer will stage a number together. In either case, the process is collaborative. "I'm very open to the choreographer being involved in my work too. I have no problem with the choreographer having things to say about my staging, even in book scenes."

McAnuff likes to have the writers involved in the process as much as possible to ensure that his vision of the show is married to theirs. For that reason, he insists on having them in attendance at rehearsal. "In *Big River* there was a whole section involving the feud. It happened in the first act of the musical. It was a relatively early section of the novel which we couldn't quite manage to solve. Finally, Bill [Hauptman, the book writer] came up with a great structural solution which was simply to eliminate it, and to move something from the second act up to take its place. It was a huge structural breakthrough. If he had been off taking a vacation in Hawaii, he wouldn't have been able to have that idea. So, you want those people, it seems to me, in the room. Or certainly close at hand."

Following a typical rehearsal day, McAnuff meets with his creative team (which, if mounting a new musical, includes the writers) to prepare for the next day's work. "It would sometimes be in my home or at a studio [around a piano], and we would then work often until two or three in the morning . . . sketching out underscoring, [or] getting a really good handle on the shape and structure of a particular section. Once I've done that work, I would gather together with my assistants—sometimes the next morning at a breakfast meeting—mapping out the staging for a particular scene, so that we go into [the next] rehearsal with a fairly strong idea of where a scene's headed, or where a production number's going." These post-rehearsal meetings continue throughout the process, through previews right up to opening night.

For all of his preparation and attention to detail prior to and during rehearsals, he admits, it often takes the preview period before a director can recognize some of the show's problems. "Oftentimes, it takes seeing the whole production working like a well-oiled machine before you can identify where you're not achieving the velocity you need to in a particular section." Even after a show enters previews, McAnuff continues to make changes. Although he notes not every problem can be solved immediately. "You have to be careful about solving problems at the right point. You can end up taking solutions that are too easy too quickly. I think you have to be cautious about panicking. Sometimes it's important to let something stew, even if it's not working terribly well, so that when you *do* solve it you're solving it permanently—you're solving the *real* problem."

Since out-of-town tryouts are mostly a luxury of the past, McAnuff develops his shows through multiple productions. *Big River*, for instance, was mounted at the American Repertory Theatre and the La Jolla Playhouse before arriving in New York, and each production (including its Broadway mounting) was substantially different than its previous incarnation. *Tommy*, as well, continued to develop from one production to the next and even beyond. "When we opened *Tommy* in New York there was something I couldn't find with the Acid Queen. The Acid Queen ends with her injecting heroin (presumably) into her system. It's a moment I hadn't been able to find until after we opened in New York. It was only when I was rehearsing the first national tour that we actually found that moment." He eventually took that moment from the national touring production and interpolated it into the ongoing Broadway run. "You carry on your work on a musical until finally nobody's going to give you the chance to do it again."

Once the show is up and running McAnuff tries to "maintain a presence at the theatre. I try to take responsibility for any replacements, I do brush up rehearsals, and I give notes from time to time." He sees maintaining a show's quality as an often difficult but important responsibility for the director, and he frequently has a number of assistants working with him who act as surrogates to oversee and maintain productions if he is unavailable. "You want to take care of these shows. You say to the actors, 'You may not be feeling great, but that's somebody's birthday present out there in the audience. To somebody, that's a really important night in their life, and something they're never going to forget.' Obviously, I'd be a hypocrite if I didn't pay them some attention to help them maintain that level."

When approaching a revival (a term he dislikes: "It sounds too much like something that happened at an accident scene"; he prefers the phrase "classic musical"), McAnuff thinks it is a mistake to be "slavishly obedient to the original production." Rather, the director must examine a classic musical with a certain amount of skepticism, realizing along the way that "certain decisions were made for the most mundane, banal reasons. And you shouldn't serve that, you should serve the greater vision of the piece. For example, if you look at *My Fair Lady* [1956; originally directed on Broadway by Moss Hart] you get these long musical sections which were used basically as interludes while they changed the scenery. That's one very practical influence on the shaping of a musical." To merely reproduce the show "as written," utilizing the stage conventions of the earlier era, says McAnuff, is not always the most effective way to tell the same story today. "You're imprisoning yourself with something that's actually quite false. You're embracing solutions to problems, rather than going back to the original material. You would never think of doing that with Shakespeare. You would never think about trying to imitate a production from 1612. The audiences would be horrified.

"That's why I like the term 'classic.' Hopefully it's a classic, or why are you bothering. Hopefully it's already relevant [to today's audience] or you wouldn't be doing it." He approaches a classic musical with the idea of giving it "a fresh look. If you don't do that, the musical doesn't really get revived. It just sort of lays there. And it feels kind of constricted by choices that were made for God-knows-what reason thirty-five years before." In his 1995 revival of *How to Succeed*, for example, the number "Cinderella Darling" was dropped from the score and replaced with a female reprise of "How To," which was deemed a better opening for act 2. The replacement of the song had "nothing to do with being 'politically correct.' To be honest, we weren't crazy about the number ['Cinderella Darling']." In correspondence with Jo (Sullivan) Loesser, Frank Loesser's widow, "She let us know that Frank hadn't been crazy about the number either." With her permission, the change was made, not to update or make the piece more relevant to present-day audiences, but to more fully meet the goals of the original text.

McAnuff believes that it is getting more and more difficult to develop work in New York City due to its "gossipy" environment. Meanwhile the luxury of taking a new show on the road for fine-tuning is rare. Therefore, he sees the regional/resident theatre system in America (of which the La Jolla Playhouse is a part) as an extremely viable place to initiate the development of new musicals. "I like to think resident theatres are good places to do creative work, and there's generally more protection in that environment from critical pressures." Additionally, he finds the commercial theatre of Broadway to have more strings attached to the artist, which he personally finds limiting. "Once you start working in the halls of commerce, there's generally a great deal of scrutiny and nervousness about everything you're doing because people's reputations and careers are on the line, and there's often a good deal of financial risk."

As artistic director of the La Jolla Playhouse, McAnuff also served as producer for many productions. He views that particular job as being an important facilitator for the creative process. "The ideal situation for a producer is that you have a creative team that you really trust, and a leader (in the director) that you can completely depend on. And in that case, your job is to nurture, and to create an environment, to produce a membrane that these artists can exist in . . . where they can work freely and comfortably at the maximum level of their ability. The best producers, in my experience, have been people who create that kind of environment, and who cast very well, in other words, cast the director and the team properly." There are, however, times when he believes a producer must become more "hands-on" in their work if the production goes off course, since they are directly responsible (along with the director) for the entire production.

He very much sees a place in the theatre for critics, believing that a "strong critical scene is extremely important" in order to preserve standards and quality. The press can often benefit the theatre, and he points to the reviewers of Southern California who covered his early work at La Jolla as having a great deal to do with securing a place for that theatre: "Because we were doing work that was often quite controversial . . . even when the critics were devastating—there was still a good deal of encouragement for the kind of work we were trying to do." McAnuff has observed a steady decline in American print journalism in the past decade, which he regards as detrimental to the theatre. "There aren't that many serious critical chairs left in the country, where a critic really has a chance to digest something and write seriously." Ultimately, he believes the words of a critic should never replace the criticism directors impose on themselves. "If you get too busy defending yourself from critics, you can forget to do the most important kind of critical work, which is the kind you do yourself."

Overall, McAnuff believes the most important realization the director of the musical needs to accept is that he or she is one of the *creators* of the work, not merely the stager of it. "I don't mean that in terms of egotism; I mean it in terms of responsibility. You have to accept the fact that you are key to the decision making as a dramatist. I think on a musical, the lyricist, the book writer, the composer, the director, and maybe the choreographer, as a group—they are the dramatist. And you are central to that process. You can't simply serve the [musical] the way you might a new play. I think it's naïve to think you can just stage a musical and come up with anything worthwhile. You're just never going to be able to do it. You are ultimately responsible for a vision, and anything less than a vision is probably not going to be enough." He elaborates on director JoAnne Akalaitis's description of the director as an *aesthetic general.* "You're a storyteller [but] you're not only responsible for your own creativity, you're responsible to support all of those other people, and to make sure that they're creating a universe together. I think aesthetic general is a damn good description of the job, and it also alludes to a war being fought, which has been my experience with what's going on with a musical. You're fighting time, you're fighting fatigue, and you're going for some kind of victory."

Mike Ockrent

Mike Ockrent comes to Broadway from England. Born in London and raised in the "English theatre tradition," he has directed numerous West End productions including the 1987 revival of Stephen Sondheim's *Follies*, which received an Olivier Award for best musical of the year. Ockrent was first represented on the New York stage in the early-'80s with plays such as *Once a Catholic*, *Educating Rita*, and the Rowan Atkinson revue *Atkinson at the Atkinson* before mounting the Broadway musicals *Me and My Girl* (1987), *Crazy for You*

All quotes are taken from personal interviews conducted by the author with Mr. Ockrent.

(1992; a remake of the 1930 Gershwin musical *Girl Crazy*), the Maltby/Shire musical *Big* (1996), and the annual Madison Square Garden musical version of *A Christmas Carol* (director and co-author; first presented in 1994).

Ockrent holds a bachelor's degree in physics from Edinburgh University. Although he cannot speak for the American university system, he cites the British system as being the best track into the professional English theatre: "I think it's the only place people can get experience and learn and practice. Certainly for me it was the way I entered the business; doing plays whilst studying physics." He did not study acting and has no experience as an actor, which he does not look upon as a detriment. "The English crop of directors, of which I'm one, I don't think any of us started out as actors. We all came in through the university system as pure directors. That I think is one of the big differences" between how American and British directors develop. He does not feel a director needs practical acting experience in order to be an effective director, unlike the typical career path of the choreographer, for example. "I think it's different for choreographers because it's such a specialist's art. You really have to be a dancer first. Whereas I think as a director you certainly don't have to come in as [an actor first]. I mean, anybody can be a director if you've got the right frame of mind and can think straight. I don't think it's brain surgery." Although he can read music to a limited degree, he does not believe this ability either is necessary for a director of musicals. In his case, "It doesn't really come into play."

Ockrent recognizes two main influences on his work in the musical theatre: the movie musicals of Busby Berkeley, and the work of Harold Prince. "Those great old movie musicals [of Berkeley's] I think are masterpieces of structure." Understanding structure he believes is one of the most significant tools a director of musicals can possess. "The one important thing without which all else fails is structure. You absolutely have to have that right to begin with. At least you've got to believe you've got it right. It's amazing how [many] people working forget that basic rule, or have no sense of that rule [and end up with] sprawling shows that have no sense of structure. It's the one thing you try and constantly be aware of." He carries that sense and understanding of structure with him and attributes it to Berkeley. Structure, however, must be balanced with content, and that he learned from Prince. "I think that the great strength of Hal's work—and it continues to be his strength—is his deep understanding of content over form. That's not really true, he has plenty of form too. But what he really understands is content. What you so often see in musicals is content deficit. Growing up in the English theatre scene content is prima facie importance to us." For Ockrent, structure and content, along with form (the way in which the story is told), make up the trinity of quality theatre. "You can have wonderful structure and no content. You can have a wonderful content and no structure. [But] I think it really works best when it all goes together: you have form, content, and structure all supporting each other in the building."

Ockrent thinks directors work best when they have "passion" for the work at hand. Additionally, he feels directors should have a personal connection with the material. "Political, sociological, philosophical, whatever it is. You have to believe in [it]. You must. There's no point in working on something for two or three years if it has nothing to say except to get a laugh here and a bit of applause there." Although his musicals are generally regarded as light entertainment in the current epic musical era, he contends that each has an underlying significance; perhaps not as obvious and overwhelming as the French Revolution or the sinking of an ocean liner, the pieces nonetheless are more than mere fluff. "Even if it isn't flashing a message at people, as the director, I know what is underneath. It's really what in the end gives underground strength to any material, that it's about something and not just flip."

He admits that during the course of his career he has at times taken on shows for which he did not have that passion. But he suggests that choosing a project because one is interested in working with a particular actor or producer, instead of based on the merits of the material itself, is ultimately unfulfilling. "Afterwards you bitterly regret it because the show is not about working with an actor or working with a producer, it's about what goes up on the stage." When he approached *Crazy for You,* the idea alone elicited his passion: "The attraction of working on an original Gershwin musical was too tempting."

His method of working as a director has continued to evolve during the course of his career, but Ockrent does not believe "what you see up on the stage stylistically has really changed." Because of this he has an unintentional signature quality to his productions: "People always tell me they can recognize my shows." He believes this characteristic is inherent in every director's work. "I think what we do as directors is tend to impose our personality on whatever production it is, and not only the director but everybody's personality impregnates the work." The combination of contributing philosophies and approaches is what makes each production unique.

Ockrent approaches the directing of a musical differently than he does a play. "They're completely different animals. They're not comparable really in any way. Directing a musical is a collaboration between at least a half a dozen very intense, creative people; masters in their own field: musical directors, choreographers, composers, lyricists, designers. So, you're really team leading, concept leading. With a play it's really a one-on-one relationship between you—if it's a new play—and the writer, and that's it." To incorporate and coordinate all the various components and personnel, he believes the director mounting a musical must be more imaginative than when mounting a play. "A straight play is often one set, two sets. It involves the machinations of eight, maybe ten characters—or maybe just one or two characters." The scale of the musical, however, is quite a bit larger. "A musical can be built and rebuilt, cut and recut, structured and restructured in so many different ways that the more imaginative you are in your approach to it, the better it is."

Defining the path the creative team will take, and then being "consistent to that idea," is, for Ockrent, one of the key functions the director performs. "The prime rule is: What is it about? I don't mean, 'It's about this guy . . . ' I mean, it has to have a spine." Once the director assesses that spine, he or she must then continuously assess the work of the collaborators against it to insure the creation of a single piece of art. "You must measure every moment against that basic line that runs through it. It has to be about what it's about. Always." Establishing a work's spine and censoring for inconsistencies, Ockrent believes, is a part of the director's job in both plays and musicals. But he contends, "It's tougher in a musical because you've got many elements," which can too easily stray from the single point of view (not often a problem with a play). "The composer's a hugely powerful creative force, the lyric writer is a hugely powerful creative force, the book writer is a hugely powerful creative force, the choreographer, [etc.]. . . . It needs one unifying narrative structure to keep these people going down one path." And no matter how talented the director might be, Ockrent suggests that once the project strays from the path, it is rarely able to be rescued. Defining the spine of the work and keeping that goal in focus help prevent such a calamity.

Establishing the structure of a musical is often a daunting task (for either the director or the writers). It is for this reason, Ockrent believes, that most musicals are based on preexisting source material. "You rarely read a play that's been adapted from a book. Musicals nearly always are an adaption. And when they're not they're often in trouble." He sees the inherent structure in a source material (whether it is used fully, or merely as a springboard for a new structure) to be tremendously beneficial as a road map for the many collaborators to follow. Such was the case with the musical *Big*, which remained fairly faithful to the film's plotline and themes. Unfortunately, in this particular case, that fidelity may have been partially responsible for the show's early demise. "I think there were too many comparisons with the movie. It didn't have Tom Hanks in it, so somehow or another [the public surmised] it was an inferior product. People felt it was trying to capitalize on the movie [or] that we were doing this to commercialize FAO Schwarz. It's a false notion of the way we do shows. We really thought we were doing a rites-of-passage story." This potential *Bye Bye Birdie* (1960) of the '90s closed after a mere 193 performances.

Although he would prefer it otherwise, he admits that the director usually takes on the responsibility of being the final editor of the script and score. "In the best of all possible worlds it's done jointly [with the writers]. It's led by the director, sometimes it's led by a writer, [but] it should be collaborative in that you all agree this number should be cut, or that scene should be changed, or twenty minutes needs coming off the show. Often the director will say, 'Here are my suggestions,' and the writers argue about it, or agree, or whatever. You become the team leader. And the stronger you are, normally the better experience it is for everybody. Provided they agree with you." He does not believe it is the director's job to *reinterpret* a writer's work, but rather to interpret the text for what it is, and then give suggestions when necessary to best illuminate the writer's original intentions. "I've grown up in the English tradition of wanting to serve your playwrights. And protect your playwrights, and protect your composers and your lyricists. Serve them to the best of your ability. It's their baby, their show. Make their work shine. That's what I enjoy doing." For Ockrent, the nucleus of every project begins with the writer. "A playwright has locked himself in his garret with his word processor, and he has a strong notion of what this is about and what it should be. Through lots of discussions, detailed questioning, you try to come to grips with exactly what it is he wants to say, what's in the back of his mind, and why he's written the play." When directing a musical this process merely expands in scope to allow for the additional contributions of the composer and lyricist.

He has learned through experience to trust the material on its own terms, rather than alter it into something it is not. With *Me and My Girl*, for example, a show originally labeled too British for American audiences, Ockrent chose to play on the show's Britishness, rather than try to extricate it from the script. He attributes the success of that show partly to a mistake he made two years earlier when mounting the "Americanized" version of his British hit *Educating Rita*. "I did [*Educating Rita*] here with Lucie Arnaz and Larry Luckinbill, and we tried to Americanize it. Rita now, instead of coming from Liverpool, was a girl from Queens, and the college was set in Queens, and so on. It didn't work because it was wrong thinking on our part. The whole structure of *Educating Rita* was firmly embedded in the British class structure, which, without the class underpinning the story, just didn't work. Very soon after that we came to be doing *Me and My Girl*, which is all about the class structure. And so, as a result of the experience of trying to make *Educating Rita* work for American audiences, my feeling, which I really expressed strongly to everybody, was *Me and My Girl* works *because* of its Britishness. If you start trying to tamper with that you risk throwing the baby out with the bath water, because you're destroying what made it work to begin with."

Additionally, he points out that each musical is different, and the rules and methods used in one production may not necessarily be applicable to the next. The book musicals of the '40s and '50s need a slightly different approach than the concept musicals of the '70s, which in turn require a different method than the epic musicals of the '80s and '90s. "If it's a sung-through musical it has a whole different shape, a whole different way of working. You can't cut it down in the same way you can cut a regular book musical, [where] you can cut scenes in half and rewrite [to tie pieces together]. But if it's a sung-through score—if the score's got twenty-five songs in it—the only thing you can really do is cut a whole song, in which case the whole glue goes out of it. So, how do you cope with that? Maybe you cut a verse here, but then the song structure goes." There are no easy and fixed answers that apply to every show.

He classifies himself as neither a permissive nor dictatorial director, but rather as "collaborative." Whether with actors, writers, or designers, "I always feel you get the best work out of people by allowing them to work at their optimum ability." He believes that comes from a collaboration that allows for their input and contribution to the overall piece of art. "It's like conducting an orchestra: you don't tell the guy how to play the bassoon. You hire the best bassoonist and allow him to interpret it." Ockrent's receptiveness to other's suggestions, he believes, opens him up to great resources of creativity. "I listen to everybody who's involved in and loves the show, and then decide what is right and not right. If it's a good idea then we use it; if it's not, we don't." This includes the producer: "I always listen to the producers." The director-producer relationship is a unique association of "two very strong characters." Just how much power and influence the producer has over the creative aspects of a show, Ockrent admits, is often "a bartering process" between the two: "It depends on the producer, it depends on the show, it depends on the relationship the director and producer have." A good producer, he notes, will more often than not give suggestions rather than make demands: "Being *told* what to do by a producer, that rarely works any more than it would work me telling somebody, 'You have to do this,' and they don't want to do it. You can't operate like that really. And producers normally don't abuse that position. If they do, they generally fire the director and hire somebody else."

He has never gone into rehearsals without a completed libretto and score and contends he never will. "Never. Some people do. It's a mistake. You have to go into every part of the process as if you've got the most perfect material and you don't believe there could be any possible changes yet to be made to it. Because you always find there are. You shouldn't even decide on your date of rehearsals until you've got a proper script and score." Obtaining the correct balance and strength in Ockrent's trinity (form, structure, and content) takes time, and he prefers to work this out in the writing long before ever entering the pre-production phase. For Ockrent, pre-production is a time to take what has been up to that point primarily on the page and attempt to visualize it three-dimensionally on the stage. "If you haven't got it right on paper [first], the chances of you getting it right on the stage are negligible."

The two most important areas of concern for Ockrent during pre-production are casting and designing. "In the pre-production period what you do with your team—which is your team of designers (and the writers will come into play as well)—is you conceptualize the show with its physical production. So, you're casting it, which is part of the physical production. You're designing it, which is part of the physical production. Sometimes the choice of design affects the writing, so things get rewritten. Sometimes the writers get inspired by a design, or a design idea inspires another idea. So, the whole process is a very organic one. But through the whole pre-production process as you're casting and designing it, you're weaving the physical fabric of the piece." Designing appropriately for each show is sometimes a difficult task. In *Big*, for instance, the show's physical production took on a life of its own. "I think it may have been overproduced. It's a smaller story and should have been done in a much smaller way." The problem, however, lies in the fact that "you often don't know these things until after the event."

In terms of casting, Ockrent sees the audition process as "gruesome," not only for the performers but for all concerned. "Everybody loathes it. You want that to be over as quickly as possible. And you always, of course, hope that the person who next walks in the room is it—and that's it, you don't have to see anybody else." He admits that sometimes a director's preconceived ideas of what a character is, or how a character looks, can be completely overturned during auditions. "In your head you imagine this guy to be tall and slim and have an Irish accent, and then in comes this Italian who's plump, and you suddenly say, 'That's how it should have been all along!' And you completely change your idea about the way that part can be interpreted." This is what Ockrent refers to as being "open to the instinct of the moment," a willingness to reevaluate and, if necessary, change one's understanding and approach to a show. "I always think that's the real creative approach, especially for directors. And it's something you really only learn with experience and time and age. [It] is to allow the experience of the moment—whether rehearsing, auditioning, or developing—to reframe your concept of what you're doing."

In the audition, Ockrent does not put undue consideration on one aspect over another (acting, singing, or dancing), but rather casts according to the demands of each individual role. He also believes personality is important, noting that musicals quite often take a toll on a performer who cannot easily adapt and change as the work develops. "The world is divided up between actors who do musicals and actors who don't. It's a different makeup in many ways, not just in whether they can sing and dance, but whether they are psychologically compatible with rehearsals for a musical. Because rehearsing a musical is not like rehearsing a play. You're making endless changes, where you can literally switch a song from one scene to another, maybe completely rewrite an act. The demands you make on musical performers are quite different." He admits that in the course of his career he has occasionally miscast a role. In such instances he more often than not will choose to work with the person and "make the best out of it," rather than replace them, a practice he does not advocate. "I've fired very few people and I should have fired more. I think really if you make a mistake it's probably better for everybody that you recognize that mistake, and [that] people move on quickly before a lot of harm is done." There have been times, he admits, when "it was a real error [on my part] not to have fired somebody within the show at an early enough stage before it actually caused real harm to the whole process." Not only can a miscast person be detrimental to the quality of the show but he or she can also do internal damage within the company by lowering morale and confidence, and creating divisions among other cast relations. In a tight-knit organization where all are intensely working toward a common goal, "it just needs one fly in the ointment and the ointment is ruined."

Early in his career Ockrent often pre-blocked his shows on paper prior to rehearsals, a practice he now sees as unnecessary at the professional level. "When you're starting off you think that's what it's all about. Young directors think [blocking is] only about walking around on the stage and not bumping into the furniture. It isn't about that. It's about the emotional relationships that cause spacial movement. You have to understand what the scene is about first, and the emotional relationships, and the drive and the action, and what's relevant about the scene." "Age" and "courage" have long since replaced that method of pre-blocking with a more collaborative approach in which Ockrent works with the actors to find movement inherent in the text. He begins with a summation of the physical demands of a scene: "I know where a scene has to begin and end physically. I know [for example] 'she' has to come on here and then she has to go off there, and in the meantime she has to meet 'him' somewhere around here." With this "vague" outline, he then works out with the actors "what the intentions are, what the actions are, what they want from it." This is not a discussion handled while sitting around a table, but with the actors "on their feet," physically working out the blocking on stage. From that, "the blocking kind of finds its own natural physicality . . . out of what's going on in the scene, not because somebody needs to make three paces to the right or move four paces to the left."

Ockrent stages "nondance numbers" himself (ballads, for example), but prefers to turn over most of the musical staging to the choreographer. "You divvy it up—'you'll do this one, I'll do that one'—but you both know exactly what each other is going to do, so you're working hand-in-glove." Occasionally, he will contribute to the staging of a number. "If there's a comic number you might do some beats, and then the choreographer comes and actually choreographs it correctly." But generally he allows the choreographer to work independently once there is agreement about how each dance will contribute to the show. This, in turn, allows Ockrent time to work on other areas of the production simultaneously.

One technique he likes to include in his rehearsal process, if time permits, is the incorporation of research assignments for the cast. He believes getting familiar with the background of a piece, whether it is a straight play or a musical, a light comedy or a heavy drama, adds layers to a show's depth and increases the company's investment in the production. For instance, "When we [did] *A Christmas Carol* at Madison Square Garden we had a lot of information on the period, and the historicity of the period, and Dickens, and so on. I have a system of giving each of the actors an aspect of their own character to go and do some research into. So, if somebody is playing, say, a servant in a country estate, they would go off and find information about servants in 1880; useful information: what they wore, how they lived, what they were paid. And then we would sit around the table and they would share this information with everybody else. You build up a picture of a period and a time and a place. The actors normally enjoy doing that." By transforming the actors into a company of researchers, Ockrent succeeds in giving his casts great sums of information upon which to draw. "More often than not we've used stuff that people dredged up from some old magazine or old book. It just enriches the show." An added advantage that comes from this type of investment and sharing is the way in which the company bonds: "It becomes much more an ensemble. People feel they're a part of a bigger process and not just on their own."

Although he is not always afforded the luxury, he prefers taking a show out of town to work out the details of a production, rather than hold previews on Broadway. "[New York] is no town to open a show cold in," noting that it is difficult enough to open a show there even *after* fine-tuning it on the road. Making changes to a show while in previews is a delicate matter, and Ockrent incorporates them strategically throughout so as to not overwhelm the cast. Planning the incorporation of changes according to importance, resources, and time is the key. "At some point when the show is going wrong, it's very good to have a kind of coherent view of what you want to do about it—a strategy. And you kind of run down that list of changes all the way through as you're going on." Too many large changes at once can often send the show into a tailspin. "You try and avoid dealing with Bosnia one night and India the next night. The actors can't take it. Nor is it possible. You're dealing with a big machine." Any change often requires the contributions of a number of people simultaneously: orchestrators, choreographers, designers, and writers, in addition to the cast and crew.

Once the show has opened, Ockrent and his assistants "pay a lot of attention to it. We pride ourselves on maintaining shows in the best possible shape." To do this he works together with a quality stage manager to prevent the show from straying from its original goals. The key is to eliminate changes and problems as soon as they arise. "It really becomes an editing process more than anything else. It's that you start removing stuff that has started to come in." A natural transference occurs during the run of a show; the actors take ownership of the production. Ockrent finds this to be a healthy development, but admits it makes maintaining the show's original intent a bit more difficult. "[I'll say to them,] 'Why are you crying there? You never did before.' And they'll say, 'I've always done that.' They didn't, but they *think* they did. Because a strange thing happens, the actors begin to think they've done the whole show on their own. Which is fine." When it comes to cast replacements, Ockrent always puts in new leading players himself. He has at times also put in chorus replacements. Although he will most often have a stage manager give replacements the basic blocking before he comes in to rehearse with them: "You can't remember the blocking, so somebody has to take them through that."

He strongly believes there is a place for critics and reviewers in the theatre. "You can't help but usually take critics seriously. I take critics seriously," particularly Frank Rich of the *New York Times*. "I always thought Frank Rich's reviews were very accurate, even when he was foul to me. I always thought he was, in retrospect, generally right." However, Rich is the exception. In general, Ockrent believes the level of criticism in New York is "appalling." This outlook stems from a belief that too much criticism and review is based on gossip surrounding a show. "You so often read a review that begins with a phrase like, 'Well, given the number of workshops this show has gone through, and the number of changes that have been made over the years . . . ' and then goes on to review it. That's irrelevant. He shouldn't even know about it. You have to deal with the work as a piece of art. If it doesn't work, it doesn't work, but review it accordingly. You can't base a review around Broadway gossip."

Although he has never begun a show in the American regional theatre system, he has often begun shows outside of London before making his way to the West End with them such as he did with *Me and My Girl*. The difference between the two systems is Britain's generously supported "subsidized" theatre. "You have a much more sophisticated subsidy base [there]." He believes the professional theatre in the United States can very much benefit from the contributions of regional theatres and points to the Roundabout Theatre, a "regional" (L.O.R.T.) theatre located in New York City, as a bridge between the two. "Commercial theatre needs its Roundabout Theatre. I think places like the Roundabout have done an enormous amount to break down that barrier [the 'no-go areas' between subsidized theatres, out-of-town theatres, and commercial theatres] which when I first came here was insurmountable."

Ockrent points out that when it comes to opening a show on Broadway, "you're going to do your best version of the show for New York," but an altered approach to that very same show may come about when mounting the national tour. "[It's] an inevitable function of the tour having to be a much smaller version of the show. You always rescale it down. You can't tour these [large] shows." These tours often begin with an entirely new series of pre-production meetings, making the show (the cast size, the scenic designs, and so forth) economically feasible for the road. "And to do that you have to try and reinvent the show often." Rescaling and redesigning the original scenic elements (usually designed around the specific Broadway theatre in which the show opens) is frequently the most daunting task. "A clever designer will actually design the touring version of the show so that it adapts to whatever house it's playing. What you often do is have a means of scaling a show down to the specific houses by bringing in the proscenium arch, or expanding the proscenium arch in some way. The designer will ask the producer, 'What's the smallest house we're going to play?' The producer will tell him which it is, and then everything is worked out from that." The tour will also occasionally provide an opportunity to incorporate changes in the fabric of the show, changes that may not have been interpolated into the Broadway production for one reason or another. "You'll often rework the show . . . fix this and fix that. You might even put in a new song or two."

Ockrent's overall approach to the musical remains flexible and open in an effort to customize his directing style to the demands of the material. At the same time, however, he keeps a keen eye on two major areas of concern, the first of which is structure. By recognizing the appropriate structure for a show and integrating that into the writing, the director will then obtain the first major goal: quality material with which to work. Structure is the means to this end and is the most important area of directorial management. The other area of concern is to "get the right cast and work with the best people." Here he refers not only to hiring the best company of actors but also to hiring the best team of collaborators. If the director works diligently to develop quality material but then hires an inappropriate choreographer, a weak musical director, or second-rate designers, then he or she has greatly limited the creative possibilities of the production. These two aspects—structure and casting/hiring—are directorial keys to success.

"I guess it's a bit like being an architect. What does an architect do? He puts up buildings. What does a musical stager do? He does musicals. But an architect will probably say to you, 'Well, it depends on if it's an office or a little house; it depends on whether it's for $5,000 or $500,000; it depends on whether I'm building it in Manhattan or in the Everglades.'" The same holds true for the director of musicals. Part of the challenge is recognizing the differences inherent in each project. Different problems (and even similar problems from one show to the next) often require different solutions. The director who is both imaginative and flexible tends to have the greatest number of available options.

Ockrent believes the best way to learn how to direct the musical is through tangible experience directing musicals. "Do it. Study structure and then do it. Anywhere. Just work out how it's done. Because so much of it is the psychology of working with people. You really can only learn how to do it by actually doing it and seeing what works and what doesn't work, and what works for you." From the repetition of mounting musicals a director will "fall into particular styles, methods, and ways of working," creating a directorial philosophy unique unto the artist.

Tom O'Horgan

Tom O'Horgan is the director of two landmark musicals: *Hair* (1968), the first fully realized American concept musical; and *Jesus Christ Superstar* (1971), the precursor to the epic-musical era of the '80s and '90s. Additionally, he has been represented on the Broadway musical stage with the revue *Inner City* (1971), and the musicals *Dude* (1972), and *Sgt. Pepper's Lonely Hearts Club Band on the Road* (1974). Among his many other Broadway credits is the Julian Barry play *Lenny*, based on the life of comedian Lenny Bruce.

All quotes are taken from personal interviews conducted by the author with Mr. O'Horgan.

Originally from Chicago, O'Horgan the actor made his way to New York in the early 1960s where he worked for a few years with such "wonderful crazy people" as Mike Nichols, Elaine May, and Paul Sills as a member of the Second City improvisation group. Following the assassination of President John F. Kennedy in 1963, he recalls, "Humor, improvisation, the whole thing ended just like that." Around that same time O'Horgan's mother passed away, an event that launched him into a "very traumatic" period of questioning. When he emerged from his depression six months later he was determined to do work that was different. "I started doing sort of strange pieces that were kind of like 'happenings,' things of that nature." When he was rebuked by a director with more traditional values for wasting his talent on frivolous experiments, he thought, "I must be on the right track."

Although he was the first choice to direct *Hair*, O'Horgan was not the first director to mount the show. (The original Off-Broadway production presented by Joseph Papp at his then-new New York Shakespeare Festival/Public Theatre was directed by Gerald Freedman.) "In the beginning of *Hair* I knew Gerry and Jim [Ragni and Rado, co-authors of the work] and they said, 'We have this great show we want you to do.' I said, 'Well, as it happens I'm leaving tomorrow for Europe with the La Mama troupe, so when I get back we'll talk about it and see.' When I got back it was at Joe Papp's, and I went to see it and I couldn't make any sense out of it. And they were very disappointed with it because Joe was a wonderful businessman, but he was a terrible meddler, and his hands were all over it." But Ragni, Rado, and composer Galt MacDermot were determined to transfer the show to Broadway. "Nothing had ever moved from Off Broadway to Broadway at that point. Never. I didn't think anything would happen."

The production at the Shakespeare Festival had only two-thirds of the score that would eventually be heard on Broadway, lacked the infamous nude scene, and was performed by "glossy-print kids" who had "no connection with [the material]." Although Broadway audiences were unaccustomed to nudity on stage at that time, O'Horgan was determined to incorporate it. "You get on a gig and you've got to make it happen. And the truth of the piece was that the hippies, which were certainly not an endangered species at that time, *did* sit-ins, and they *would* take their clothes off. It was a very natural kind of thing to do at that time. We had nude scenes in everything we did. It was no big deal. And nobody thought anything about it. Stuff I did at La Mama, in small theatres, in a church down[town], we always had nude scenes." O'Horgan saw *Hair* as just another experimental work in a long line that dominated the small, Off-Off-Broadway scene at that time, an extension of "the stuff we were doing for the last decade before that. What was at the Public had very little to do with the movement we were all involved in."

Meanwhile, producer Michael Butler transferred the show from the Shakespeare Festival to the unconventional Cheetah, a New York City discotheque that served as a way station between the Papp production and Broadway. During that time "Bertrand Castelli, who was the executive producer, and Gerry and Jim and Galt came to me quite separately [and asked me] to take over the piece." O'Horgan agreed, revising the show for Broadway: "I never thought for two seconds it would last on Broadway. I thought what we were doing was a sit-in. I thought we were going up to this plaster palace, and [we'd] sit down, be there a minute, and they would get rid of us—but we would have made a statement." When the show turned out to be a success, nobody was more shocked than O'Horgan.

O'Horgan never learned how to direct from any one person. Being a child actor exposed him to a great many methods and from that he developed his own approach. "I started working in the theatre as a child. So, it's been that kind of absorption of being with people and working with different directors. But then I got involved deeper with music [he holds a master's degree in the field] and worked with a lot of musical people. I just was never very happy with the way people went about their work. So, I suppose I just evolved a style of my own." This style was influenced by a number of forces, a significant one being his father. "My father wanted to be in the theatre desperately and his parents wouldn't let him, so he insisted on me." This insistence came in the way of exposing O'Horgan to the vast diversity of the theatre at an early age. "When I was a kid my father took me to see *Madame Butterfly*. It was the first opera I ever saw. He didn't like opera very much; he said it sounded like a maternity ward to him but thought I should see it." O'Horgan saw a great many musicals as a child as well, including shows featuring Olsen and Johnson, two Vaudevillians who had a string of successful revues during the '30s and '40s: "These were people who were really some kind of vaudeville dadaists. They just did the weirdest, most wonderful, audience participation stuff. So, a lot of things that I really felt were reinforced by these people." Additionally, his father's interest in magic and magicians instilled in him an interest in illusion: "The concept of illusion—stage illusion—has always been fascinating to me." But perhaps O'Horgan's greatest influence came from the movie musicals of Busby Berkeley. "As a child I had seen those movies . . . *42nd Street* and things like that. Those incredible production numbers, that kind of sculptural aspect that Busby was able to do . . . I know that they meant something to me." In the same way in which Berkeley used large choruses to create his visually impressive overhead kaleidoscope formations, O'Horgan too uses his casts "sculpturally" to create stunning visual effects.

O'Horgan's visual expressiveness and creative staging can be seen throughout his career, although perhaps it is no more clearly illustrated than in the ascension of Christ in *Jesus Christ Superstar*. "I thought: How to do *Superstar* so it doesn't look like something painted on black velvet?" He draws inspiration from a variety of sources. In this particular case, inspiration came from a documentary. "I had seen—and I never told anybody this at that time—a documentary about insects." This film would help shape his entire concept for the show. "The view that I took was that this was a reenactment of the Christ story by a future, future, future group of people who are really insects. So, if you look at the costumes of the priests, for instance [designed by Randy Barcelo] they really are some kind of insect. You see that through the whole piece." This was not a concept he shared with the cast. "Sometimes you have these ideas, and you don't have to tell anybody about it, but it's something that makes things happen. And you and the designers sort of share this [between yourselves]." At the transformation of Christ, Jesus appeared "ensconced in various kinds of materials and wire structures and so forth," moving slowly heavenward on a hydraulic lift built into the stage. As he ascended, "people came up and took pieces off of him. As he got higher more pieces came off." Once he reached the ultimate height, a great gold cape unfurled from Christ, draping and spreading across the entire stage. "What it really was was a butterfly coming out of a chrysalis. If you came to see it you wouldn't necessarily [recognize it as such], you'd just think, 'It's something I know, but I don't know what it is,'" something simple and familiar which invokes a sense of "mystery."

O'Horgan has been involved in musicals throughout his life. Early in his career he worked as a performer, composer, and writer. "Then I began playing the harp in order to make a living. I did a musical where I played the harp—a beatnik harpist—and read poetry." As a director he finds this performance experience invaluable. "I think what's important for a director of any kind is to have the need to perform and want to make performance," and understand what that is from a performer's point of view. "The thing about theatre, whether it's musical theatre or whatever, is the 'moment.' It's like jazz, it's like improvisation. It's the moment that counts. It's not like something that's in a can or on a cassette where you can just feed it into a machine and it plays [the same way over and over]. The 'moment' is never the same, and particularly in musicals so much is involved with the human body dancing and singing." Ironically, for all his musical theatre experience and education he had a long wait before he was offered his first musical to direct. "When I first started directing back in the '60s, nobody ever thought of me doing a musical. I did all these straight plays, wonderful plays. Sam Shepard's early plays, Lanford Wilson, people like that, [but] I never could get anything musical. Then, of course, I did *Hair* and they wouldn't let me do straight plays anymore!"

For O'Horgan, the essence of the theatrical event is the performance, an "experience" shared between the performers and the audience; and anything that heightens that experience and makes it more real is thus more relevant. "It seems to me in the theatre if you slavishly build a kitchen sink, that's about as unreal an idea as you can get to. Whereas Kabuki is a thousand times more real for me. I think that all early theatre, world theatre, is more relevant than most of the stuff they're doing now. That's why I'm not exactly conversant with what's going on on Broadway. For me, it's a dark age. I just think that all of this revival—it's lovely to see these old pieces again—but let's write something new. And then when they *do* write something new, it's just sort of a weird copy of a bad piece. The authors of what we have now are the Shuberts and the Nederlanders and people like that [who] have made Broadway into some kind of place for bridge-and-tunnel people, and foreign people who come here. None of my friends ever go to Broadway. It just doesn't speak to them."

Experimentation in the theatre, of which O'Horgan is a longtime advocate, is a much smaller world than it was in the '60s and '70s with the rise of the Off-Off-Broadway movement. Fewer theatres are involved in the type of risk taking O'Horgan pioneered; however, that does not keep him from his work. Often he will mount shows and readings in his own New York City apartment where he has erected a stage in his living room. "We *do* exist out there, it's just there's no community of it. When I go to BAM [the Brooklyn Academy of Music] or places like that where they do experimental pieces, I see the people I know. When I go to Broadway, I'm sitting with strangers." There was a time when Broadway embraced O'Horgan's form of experimentation, but economics have long since forced his work into smaller venues.

O'Horgan approaches directing plays and musicals in the same manner. For him, there is no difference between the two. "I don't really think in terms of 'musical theatre' and 'not musical theatre.' I really don't. I think the major problem with most straight plays today is that they have no rhythm nor musicality. I don't mean putting music to them or anything of that sort. I mean, just the sense of the way scenes break, and the action happens, the speed, the tempi." Finding the rhythm and music inherent in a work, whether a straight play or musical, is vitally important to him. "I'm a musician, and I have a firm belief that musicians basically talk another language. They speak in notes, or they speak in metrics and pitches and rhythms. And so when I direct a play it's as much a musical event: the orchestration of the voices of the people you choose, and the way they move, the sculptural aspect of it like dance and so forth. I approach singing in the same way I would approach a monologue." Because of that, his straight plays often include a good deal of music. "I'll always remember doing *The Tempest* once in Philadelphia, and I'm walking out and this woman said, 'Why did he put all that music in there?' *The Tempest* is a wonderful musical. It has some great speeches in it, but it also has some wonderful songs and pantomimes and magic and dancing. [Theatre is] about an appointment between two groups of people, and whether they sing or dance or speak or jump up and down or do acrobatics doesn't really matter to me."

Shows that lack rhythm and musicality, O'Horgan says, are usually "boring as hell. This is often the case with directors who are not musical. They just don't feel that sense of composition. I always had music in my plays, but they were not musicals. Everything I've done in the straight-play world has been influenced by music. That's what makes my pieces the way they are; whether it's good, bad, or indifferent there is that quality to them. Being a composer and singer my approach may be somewhat different than somebody who comes at it from a dance background or something." He believes that "the musical aspect, the pyelic rhythmic aspect" is inherent in every play and must be dealt with, not ignored, by the director. This holds true for the musical as well, a form that in addition to having an *inherent* musicality and rhythm, incorporates the use of music, singing, and dance, which more fully develops these inherent qualities.

Along with plays and musicals, O'Horgan directs quite a bit of opera; however, he does not approach it in an "experimental" or avant-garde way. "You have to approach opera more traditionally. The singers are trained in a completely different way," and productions are generally rehearsed in a different fashion. The director attempting to mount an opera (a term equally applied to works spanning a 400-year period, numerous countries, and several languages and cultures), O'Horgan suggests, should not approach each similarly. "Opera's a historic form. It's like a museum [in that] you have all these different periods. So, obviously, an early opera by Monteverdi or someone like that, can't be done the same way you do a Verdi opera, or a very modern piece like *Wozzeck*. You can't. They're all completely different." Epic musicals (such as *Jesus Christ Superstar*), which border on opera in form, are different still because they require "a different kind of singer." Recognizing the era in which the piece is written and understanding the influences spawning the work are important tools for the director mounting an opera. Ironically, his ability to read music is not seen as one of those tools. "In opera, the conductor is king. Always has been.

And most conductors are not interested in a stage director who can read music or has any musicality at all, because they feel threatened. I don't want to fight that battle." Being a classically trained musician no doubt accounts for his conclusion that "the kind of stuff I was involved in [with] *Superstar* is closer to where I really am than the stuff in *Hair*. *Superstar* was, in a sense, an opera."

He feels it is vitally important that the director make some personal connection with the play or musical he or she directs in order to bring it properly to life on the stage. "I read a play, and for me there is a sound that comes to me, and a smell, and a color. And out of that everything else is born. I think any director, particularly in musicals, [has] to look at a script and get an aroma from it, a certain sense, or a hum, or a taste, or something. It's not definable in so many terms. If you don't have that, if it doesn't just sort of jump off the page [and speak to you]" you probably should not direct it. "You have to pick a piece that you really relate to, otherwise it's so much carpentry." From that particular sense or aroma or color or sound, the piece itself will guide the director to the proper style of presentation, the proper cast to assemble, and the proper designers to hire.

For O'Horgan auditioning is the most important task the director accomplishes during pre-production. "I've always said, my whole life has been auditioning. Finding people is one of the most important ventures. I think you have to be really in love with finding talent. Because, as most musicals are today, everybody plays lots of parts. Therefore you have to find people in the ensemble who are really capable of doing that." At the same time, the audition process itself is not one of the most pleasant aspects of the job: "It's the ugliest and most inhumane practice that I can think of, and I try to think of other ways of doing it," but to no avail. He tries to look beyond the nervousness of the auditioner and give each the time necessary to present themselves to the best of their ability. "You've got to be able to sit there and listen, and give them the chance to do something. Sometimes a person will be just bloody awful, and [yet] there's something there. And then, after you've let them squander a couple of minutes, they suddenly relax and they do something for you, and you're in love with this person for the rest of it. That's happened to me over and over again." He notes that casting directors can be useful to a limited degree as long as they know exactly what the director is looking for in the first place. Other times you simply get lucky: "The best people I've ever found—Ben Vereen, Andre De Shields—are people who just walked in off the street." Casting *Hair*, due to its ensemble of hippie characters and its true rock 'n' roll score (a novelty for Broadway at the time) had its own unique problems. "Nobody knew what we wanted. People would come and they were all short-haired and singing Cole Porter. We were chasing people down the street who looked right. We went and ransacked record studios and got backup singers . . . because they knew how to sing this stuff." It was a much more lengthy and involved process than he had ever encountered, "and certainly more than we had to do later when we did *Hair* [1977 revival] because then people knew what we wanted."

He is frustrated by the lack of "real voices" in the musical theatre and traces this problem back to casting. "I love real singers, which is something we don't have because I think most of the people who are involved in casting haven't any ears on the sides of their heads. I love voices, and I love voices with range. It doesn't have to be opera, but it has to be real. It's difficult because where pop music is now is so anti-singing. One thing about rock music at its finest was that it required extraordinary voices to do it." Ironically, he feels, "amplification—which is one of the things they always blame me for—has taken over completely," making it "almost not necessary [for singers] to be able to do anything. We needed amplification because rock music is loud." But, he suggests, its continued and often unnecessary use takes away from the natural beauty of the singer's voice and the intimacy of the theatrical event. He admits assembling an ensemble is a key goal and will often cast someone who may be slightly less talented than another performer if he feels they more precisely fit into the ensemble he is trying to create. This is exemplified in his casting of *Hair*: "There were some people who had theatre experience, but ninety percent of them didn't."

He also recognizes the subjectivity of casting. For the Broadway production of *Lenny*, "a straight play (although it contained music), I looked forever to find a Lenny. The lessons you learn are very strange. I looked around and looked around, and finally found Cliff Gorman who was wonderful. [But] when his contract was up he decided to go. So, we had this other guy do it. And he was terrific, but totally different. I was, of course, a little crazed at the moment, but then I realized 'this works just as well. It's just as valid.' I think no one was any better than Cliff. All I'm saying is there are all these different people playing these roles," and though the director may cast with a specific interpretation and image in mind, the truth is that most roles are open to a broader range of interpretations than the director may initially recognize.

"Of course, also in pre-production you have to get with your writer and composer, you have to know what the score is, you have to know the ranges, you have to know what you're looking for. Then, of course, by this point you usually have a pretty firm notion (at least I usually do) of what I want the thing to be physically: lights and sets and costumes." Once designs are agreed upon, "I almost never change [my mind]." Although he takes on an improvisational approach with his actors once in rehearsal, he contends that design elements must be well thought out and set in advance. "By the time you're in your first day of rehearsal you have things starting to be built." The actors then must work around the preapproved set, and not the other way around. The physical, visual components of a show are extremely important to him, and he takes great pains to aid their development. This collaboration must balance the director's needs with the designer's creativity and ability. "You have to be able to say, 'Hey, I'm not going to build this for you, but this is sort of what I need.' And then be able to allow them to do their work. Otherwise, you cut off their stream and it just won't function right. Listen to them, and often they show you things that they had tucked away in their brains that they didn't even know they had. I think probably the whole thing [is] the ability to love to collaborate." For him, this is the key to working with not only designers but all the personnel involved in creating a show.

For O'Horgan it is not so important that he head into rehearsals with a completed script and score as long as "you have a good sense of what it's about, the basic sense of it, how it's going to lie on the stage, how it works, what the physical aspects are." With this detailed outline in mind, and a number of the larger questions answered in theory, he enjoys having a hand in shaping the show as it progresses. He admits, however, "It's not good. It's not the way to do it." Yet he contends that even with a completed script in hand, "that doesn't mean that things don't change." As long as the concept and outline are well developed at the outset, he feels the script will evolve properly. Sometimes, however, a project evolves incorrectly. Such was the case with the Ragni/MacDermot musical *Dude*. When first approached to direct the show, O'Horgan did not feel the concept was fully developed enough to even begin rehearsals. Ignoring his advice, the creators headed into production with director Rocco Bufano on board. "Then after a week or so in previews they called me to come in to try to do something. It was too late. I couldn't do anything. It was a great concept [and] the music was some of the best music that Galt had ever done. But he [Ragni] sort of got away from it. I told him how much I loved it before but it was too late; it was something else."

O'Horgan sees the director as the final editor of the script and score. His approach to editing, however, is a collaborative one with the writers. "The degree of success you have with that has to do with your degree of working with people." The director must have a persuasiveness to lead the creative team in the direction he or she deems best for the show. At the same time, in order to allow experimentation to happen, directors must be open to accept different ways of presentation, different structures, and the way different playwrights work, without forcing new pieces to conform to old rules. "Every playwright's completely different. Particularly in the period when an artist is first coming of age. That's a very free period." Editing is a very delicate job and the director must be careful not to let it get out of hand: "The problem with writers and composers is you get them into a cutting frenzy and then you have to stop them. 'Now, wait a minute, I love that part!' Then, of course, later on they do what's called the writer's revenge. They publish the piece and put everything they ever wrote in it. And then people read the script and they say, 'How do you put this damn thing on?'"

O'Horgan approaches blocking from a visual perspective. "I think theatre is sculpture, that's one of the other aspects of it. I think it has to do with moving blocks of creatures around, and what's forward and what's back, and the rapidity that things move in structures. I think directors are sculptors; they deal with kinetic theories. For me, actors are a moving sculpture." Based on elaborate and well-developed ideas, he contends he is an "improvisor" who manifests these moving sculptures while working with the actors in rehearsal. And though well prepared in his mind, he balks at the idea of preparing on paper ahead of time. "I think that stops something. Because a person walks out on stage and that person inspires you to do something different than you would ever think about." He will often incorporate the actor's ideas if they fit into the picture he sets out to create. Overall, his blocking is extremely visual, often incorporating stage illusions and unexpected visual thrills in an unconventional use of the stage space.

He usually works as his own choreographer, yet he is more apt to develop a "movement" through music than a conventional dance. This movement is often an extention of the blocking, giving his work a seam-lessness in its visual presentation. "Most of my shows have movement in every inch. If you did a labanotation of it, it would be a very big, busy book." He believes the movement of a work is either "inherent in the piece or you have to superimpose something" on the piece. In either case every show's visual expressiveness should be unique. "You have to somehow make a physical language that matches the music that you're dealing with. I think that each piece has its own kind of kinetic world that it works in, and if you don't devise that language the piece is never going to be fully blown." A show without its own movement tends to come across as old fashioned and uninspired. "If your whole group of singers don't move, then you're going to get this kind of old-fashion opera effect where [singers] come out and sing, then they go off and the dancers come out and dance a little bit. It's stupid, but there's a lot of that going on. Whereas if you find things that singers can do physically," it makes for a much richer, more fully integrated work.

If he has time during rehearsals, which he admits he often does not ("the crazier you are, the weirder the stuff you do, the less time you have to do it; that's a rule"), then he likes to engage the company in group exercises. "If I had my druthers, I'd spend a lot of time 'structur-ing' the group. That is to create a sense of group, a sense of movement, a certain kind of sound." During *Hair* rehearsals, for instance, "we always spent maybe forty-five [minutes] to an hour on just exercises. The beginning was just warm-ups [to establish] a sense of movement, which was really important." Through this series of warm-up, breath-ing, and vocal exercises, which includes theatre games and improvisa-tions, O'Horgan creates a close-knit ensemble of actors. "Our game is to take *you* and find out what *you* have to offer that no one else in the world has." Because these games are centered around the play the company is rehearsing, it gives the actors a greater understanding of the piece and its themes, and gives tangible character choices with which to experiment. This, he believes, aids the actors during long runs, giving them a certain flexibility in their interpretation within the structured repetitiveness of the performance.

By focusing on the strengths of the individual performers, his shows often reflect that particular company's personality. This, he suggests, is the reason why many of his subsequent productions vary from the original. "I did seven or eight productions [of *Hair*]—in Chicago, and then the one in L.A., and the one in London—they were all so different because of the people in them. I did *Jesus Christ Superstar* twice and they were quite different." For this reason he does not like to approach revivals as remountings of the original production. If the *original* production differs from city to city and from cast to cast, then how can a *revival* reproduce the original? For the 1977 Broadway revival of *Hair*, however, he admits, "I was sort of put-upon to do the same show at that point. Not that it was ever the same." He thinks directors should feel a freedom to take shows apart, reexamine them, and put them back together again in unique ways. "Look back in history, that's certainly the case with earlier plays and operas. Every time they did them, they did them differently." Such was the approach he took directing the Berlioz opera *Les Troyens*: "You take a lunch and a sleeping bag if you do all of it. Berlioz never saw the whole piece himself. So I, with the conductor, we just took that thing and 'fixed' it."

He believes a show is not finished once it heads into previews; on the contrary, a lot of the fine-tuning comes in front of an audience. "If you think that in four weeks or six weeks you can get something done, you can't. Most of the work in a show happens in the preview period as far as I can understand." After a show has opened, "I always stick around and drive everybody nuts. And I don't change anything particularly," but let the show evolve naturally into its own mature production. In the case of *Hair*, however, "My job after the [various productions] were open was to try to keep them down to size, because it kept growing like a fungus. *Hair* being what it was tended to go on its own if you weren't riding it all the time." On one occasion he returned to watch a performance and found the show "sort of splayed out in some weird kind of form. I came in after it had started. Of course, the people [cast] are circulating the theatre all the time, so word got back that I was there." Once the cast realized the director was present, the performance quickly retreated back into O'Horgan's original production. He enjoys putting in and rehearsing cast replacements, but he admits that, at times, it can be a difficult task. With *Hair*, for example, there was a tremendous influx of cast replacements. "*Hair* was so hard to do—physically hard and vocally hard—that people just fell by the wayside. It was hard to do that eight times a week. Nobody realizes that because everybody had such fun while we were doing it. But our mortality was extraordinary. I used to think we had a revolving door on the stage door because [new cast members] came and went with such rapidity."

As O'Horgan sees it, widespread theatrical experimentation, which once took place simultaneously on and Off Broadway, in regional theatres, and in colleges, is the only force available to combat the continual recycling of the past. However, today such adventurousness is relegated to a handful of specialty houses that refuse to be satisfied with the state of the modern theatre. He does not believe the universities allow experimentation to flourish as they once did. Nor does he see the regional theatre system as the hub for innovation and experimentation: "There are some [which take risks], but most of them are very conservative and basically in the business to please those people who put the money up to keep the place alive."

Beyond the conservativism that O'Horgan sees dominating most college and university theatre departments (which he sees as counterproductive), O'Horgan believes colleges possess very few of the necessary tools to educate artists in the first place. After a number of experiences dealing with university theatre departments and their students, he concludes, "A lot of kids who are in universities today are not the most talented people, but their parents had the money to send them— I guess to keep them off the street—and so they study theatre." Although he acknowledges that a good number of the students coming out of these college programs seem externally well trained, internally "there's no one there. These kids [are] just so empty." The irony, O'Horgan points out, is that "a lot of the kids who are really talented don't have the money to go to universities. But they want to be in the theatre." For this reason he believes, "There's got to be more places for people to do what they do, like La Mama [Experimental Theatre]." Instead of university training, he believes true development of the student-director comes from life itself and through hands-on experience. "If you want to be a dir-ector, and you want to do musicals, you should assist. The theatre's a kind of apprentice system. You learn more by working with somebody. There's a lot of work to do. Get in and learn everything about everything. I think, in a musical more than anything, you have to have your fingers in all the departments. If you don't know about lights, you're crazy. If you don't know about movement, I don't know what you're doing in the business. If you don't know about costumes, if you don't know about stage works, and so forth. . . . I think the best musical theatre is individual. It's something that you evolve." Most importantly, O'Horgan believes the director of musicals must "have a rhythm. I mean that in the broadest sense." From this is created theatre that is unique and genuine.

After attending a concert, O'Horgan refers to the musician as someone who "has nothing to say, but says it so wonderfully." In his opinion, the theatre is in a similar rut: "The times we're living in are so stoned out in some weird way that to make a real statement is almost an anathema." He recognizes that the '60s and early '70s were a turbulent time but believes there was an energy within people to produce, experiment, and play that is missing in today's artists. "It was a kind of performance we don't have now. That was a really unbelievable time. People were right on the edge. And silly or foolish as they may have been in many cases, people were involved. It was wonderful." And the music that held it all together was rock 'n' roll: "That's where the energy was at that time. I wish it was still. I wish it was *any*where now." He refers to the decade of the '60s as a "very strange monster of our time . . . an anesthetized, weird place" that created a Generation X, which is "really empty" creatively. But he believes the generation coming of age at the beginning of the new millennium holds promise. "There's a group that's coming now. It's the harbinger of something else that's going to happen."

Harold Prince

In addition to producing some of the most successful musicals of the '50s and '60s, among them *The Pajama Game* (1954), *Damn Yankees* (1955), *West Side Story* (1957), *Fiorello!* (1959), *A Funny Thing Happened on the Way to the Forum* (1962), and *Fiddler on the Roof* (1964), Harold Prince has also directed some of the most influential musicals in Broadway history, including *Cabaret* (1966), *Company* (1970), *Follies* (1971; co-directed with Michael Bennett), *A Little Night Music* (1973), *Pacific Overtures* (1976), *Sweeney Todd* (1979), *Evita* (1980),

All quotes are taken from personal interviews conducted by the author with Mr. Prince.

Merrily We Roll Along (1981), *Phantom of the Opera* (1988), *Kiss of the Spider Woman* (1993), and *Parade* (1998), among a host of others.

Prince, who is arguably the most important director in the history of the American musical theatre, initially had aspirations of being a playwright. While a student at the University of Pennsylvania, however, he quickly realized where his strengths lay. "I wrote one play and directed it. I got the directing award, not the playwriting award. I reasoned very quickly that I wasn't going to be the best, and decided to stop that." But what Prince took with him from that initial foray into playwriting was the sense that "being able to put words together must be useful to a director." Once out of college, he sent off a teleplay of his to the office of George Abbott, who in the late-'40s was dabbling in experimental television. "Attached to the script was a note saying, 'I just got out of the University of Pennsylvania. I don't know what I could possibly do that would earn a nickel, so why don't you give me a job and not pay me. And if you can figure out that you're not paying me from the quality of what I do, I want you to fire me immediately.' That intrigued them, and I got a job."

Prince's goal, however, was to work in the theatre. After a year "puttering around in television," he got that chance when Abbott's stage manager, Robert Griffith, took on Prince as his assistant for the Broadway revue *Touch and Go* (1949). After working on another Abbott revue (*Tickets Please* [1950]), and then spending two years stationed in Germany during the Korean War, fate intervened. "You'll never talk to anyone who's more willing to acknowledge what an enormous part luck plays in anyone's life. And I was really lucky." During *Wonderful Town* (1953), Prince, who was again working as Griffith's assistant, was allowed to rehearse Rosalind Russell's replacement, Carol Channing. "Abbott came to see it and he said, 'You can direct!' I was just doing his direction, but he had some confidence about it." With Abbott's encouragement, Prince's sights were clearly set on becoming a director. Prince and Griffith soon after became partners. When they noticed that Abbott did not enjoy producing as much as directing, they decided they should replace Abbott as his own producer, to which Abbott agreed. Prince never wanted to be a producer, but he was not in a position at that time to strike out on his own and become a director. He saw the move as a stepping-stone closer to obtaining his goal: "Fill the breach that's there. Don't hang on obdurately waiting for the opportunity that may not come. Position yourself for the opportunity at a later date."

By 1960 word was out that Prince wanted to direct. When producer Roger Stevens, with whom Prince had worked on *West Side Story*, called and asked if he would be interested in being considered as the director of *Juno* (the Marc Blitzstein/Joseph Stein musical adaptation of O'Casey's *Juno and the Paycock*), Prince excitedly said yes. He mentioned the prospect to Griffith, who unexpectedly suggested that the two of them direct it together. Unbeknownst to Prince at that time, Griffith had harbored a long-standing desire to be a director as well. "He didn't want to see this pip-squeak kid with all this ambition do this. So, when he said, 'We could do this together,' I dropped it, and went on about my business." Out of loyalty and love for his partner, he removed his name from consideration. The following year, "I was sitting at my desk and the phone rang and someone said, 'Bobby Griffith just had a heart attack on the golf course with Abbott in Westchester and they've taken him to the hospital.' I got into a car and I drove up to the hospital and he died the next morning. It changed everything." Prince soon accepted his first professional directing job: Thornton Wilder's play *The Matchmaker* for the Phoenix Theatre.

His first musical came in 1962 when he was asked to save the troubled *A Family Affair* during its out-of-town tryout. "The phone rang and somebody said, 'We hear you're a burgeoning director. Well, we can't get Abbott, and we can't get Robbins, and we can't get [Gower]

Champion, and we can't get . . . You want to come down and look at it?'" After viewing the show, he told the creators, "'Yeah, I'll stay and work on it, but you realize it needs an enormous amount of work and it's opening in New York in two-and-a-half weeks. You've got to do everything I say. I can't debate anything. You've got to do it all and take your chances. You couldn't be any worse off than you are right now.'" The creative team agreed, and Prince was brought on board.

"Abbott said to me when I started, 'I have one piece of advice for you: Do you think this show can be a hit?' And I said, 'I don't think so.' He said, 'Just remember that, because as you start to work you're going to fall in love with it. And you don't want to be disappointed if it's not a hit.'" With that, Prince went to work changing more than half the book, painting out a good deal of the scenery, throwing out a number of costumes, and restaging the entire show. "We opened two-and-a-half weeks later on schedule, and I got a good review from Walter Kerr [critic for the *Herald Tribune*, and co-author and director of *Touch and Go*]." The show was not a success, surviving a mere sixty-five performances, but "it set me up. Lots of people had known it was a disaster and lots of people now knew that there was a young director doing good work."

Prince's approach to directing has become far less dictatorial than it was with such early shows as *A Family Affair* and *She Loves Me* (1963). "In those days . . . I was always working for an end result, rather than working in a process *towards* an end result. The end result I sort of knew. But how do you get to the end? Very often I had no idea. As the years went on I gathered more and more equipment to achieve that." One of the most important tools Prince acquired was the ability to communicate his ideas to others and, in turn, motivate actors to realize their potential. The problem for him was: How do you get an actor—an artist—with all their insecurities and vulnerabilities and talent to meet the director halfway? Or, in some cases, more than halfway? "It isn't by being a martinet." Prince finds the answer in the atmosphere he creates. "There are two kinds of directors: there are the punishers—they're people who thrive on crisis, who like contention, who make turmoil and feed off it, and create wondrously from that—and there are people who want the atmosphere to be life-affirming and fun. That's me. My shows aren't always fun, and some of my shows are very serious business, but the process of doing them is fun." Within that relaxed and creative environment, Prince believes actors do their best work.

He acknowledges the influence of two great directors on his work: George Abbott and Jerome Robbins. Abbott taught him discipline, a zero-tolerance policy for histrionics and self-indulgence, and a striving for truth beyond a shadow of a doubt. No matter what you do, no matter how farcical or funny the situation may seem, Prince believes it must be rooted in truth and it must be rooted in character. "You never slam a door to hear a door slam. You slam a door to get in or out of a room." Prince sees this to be evident in both his and Abbott's shows, though he concedes that their work could not be less alike. From Robbins, he learned dynamics and staging. "I could see the patterns that [Robbins] put on stage and how much they differed with what a director does. Directors always move actors linearly across the stage. A choreographer moves people from upstage to down. Or downstage to up. Or diagonally across the stage. And often moves them in clumps. It's thrilling. That's how I move people." To create his musicals, Prince uses this mixture of absolute truth within the book, along with "a physicalization, which has the energy that dance can give to the stage."

He does not read music and admits that being able to probably would benefit him, particularly in his work with opera. However, he suggests that most of what he does in the musical theatre is based more on his emotional "instinct about music and how it functions," rather than an educated understanding of musical theory. When it comes to editing the libretto and score, Prince believes those decisions should fall to the director. Unlike some directors who edit after the writers have completed their work, Prince works with them throughout the process, seeing himself as much a collaborator as any one of the writers. He is careful to point out, however, that the director's role as collaborator differs with each director depending upon their strengths. "Where is your strong suit? My strong suit is with text. If I were a choreographer and I got into trouble I'd probably rush right down to my feet to solve the problem. I can't do that. [I rush] to my head, to the words." In two instances, *She Loves Me* and *On the Twentieth Century* (1978), shows were brought to him already written. In most cases, however, "I work from the first day. The author and I and the designers start almost simultaneously at the starting gate," a practice he prefers over mounting revivals. "Half the fun is going from nothing to something." He contends that it is far more complicated to mount an original work for the first time than it is to mount a revival. "It's a totally different assignment. Somebody will do *Sweeney Todd* now and they will act as if it was just as complicated as something that we worked on for three years." Prince has, from time to time, directed revivals such as *Candide* (1992) and *Sweeney Todd* (1994) for the New York City Opera, and *Cabaret* (1987), *Show Boat* (1995), and *Candide* (1997) on Broadway; but even with a revival, Prince likes to "create." Regarding his Broadway remounting of *Show Boat*, for example, he says, "I would not have enjoyed it if I had just taken the existent script and score and put it on the stage. First of all, I wouldn't have done it." Though he considers himself a collaborator, he does not take authorship credit for the shows he directs. "It seems to me writers deserve writing credit." The difference between what Prince does and what his mentor George Abbott did is separated by a fine line: "Abbott wrote lines. I don't write lines." But Prince's influence and contribution is substantial, resulting in his name being included in the copyright of every original Prince production from *Company* (1971) to the present.

Working on a show he feels passionately about is one of his greatest pleasures: "That brings with it fear, trepidation, anxiety, and excitement. But if you wait to feel that way about everything you do, you will work one-third the amount of time I've worked. And I like working." He admits he has done a number of shows he did not like in order to keep busy, shows he thought "would not work in terms of reaching a wide audience, or getting the approval of critics, or even getting *my* approval. But I learned from those shows. Don't underestimate the value of working on something that isn't superior, in terms of it being a learning process." In fact, a number of times, he contends, he has had "humongous successes with shows that had 'adequate' material."

Pre-production can be a long and drawn-out process for Prince, sometimes lasting several years. However, he suggests that the director's pre-production work is the most crucial. During this time his attention focuses on the collaborative process with the writers to insure a well-structured, well-executed manuscript from which to work. He says he has never gone into rehearsals without a completed script and score; rehearsals are treacherous enough, he says, when you *do* have a completed work without the added pressure of having to finish writing the piece while in rehearsals. This is followed by an equally integrated collaboration with the designers to bring the story to life on the stage. Prince recognizes, "One of my strong suits is the visual," not only in staging but design as well. The visual element is important to him and he sees it as a part of his instinctive makeup as a director. In the same way that he is the final editor of the libretto and score, Prince sees the director as the final editor of the design elements as well. Getting the design right for a production can be a long, evolutionary process, which is why he likes to begin work with the designers, if not at the same time as the writers, then soon after. Next in importance is casting. Prince believes that it is vital to have these critical elements in place before rehearsals begin, when there is still unpressured time to correct errors in execution. To some, this may appear to limit spontaneous development during the rehearsal period; however, Prince believes otherwise, stating, "It doesn't stifle creativity . . . it protects you."

This does not mean that changes do not occur during the rehearsal process. Though the show may be labeled *complete* when rehearsals begin, he is not suggesting that the libretto is *finished*: "You always put things into rehearsal you don't have total confidence in, but the less the better." There have been times when he has made great alterations in his musicals prior to their New York openings. During rehearsals of *Cabaret*, for example, Prince was unable to get the scene he wanted when in act 2, Cliff Bradshaw arrives at the cabaret to retrieve Sally and take her home. "So I took the actors in the lobby and we ad-libbed our way through it." He showed the scene to Joe Masteroff, the book writer, who made slight alterations in it, and the scene went into the show. For the "A Weekend in the Country" number in *A Little Night Music* (a song planned for the show but still unwritten when rehearsals began), he again ad-libbed through it with the cast. He and the actors improvised a sequence involving the passing of an invitation to the country from one character to another. "Steve [Sondheim] came and saw the whole sequence unfold on stage in all its clumsiness." It was a rough outline of the scene and "very basic stuff," according to Prince, but it was enough for Sondheim who went home and wrote "A Weekend in the Country" based on it, a number that "is the opposite of very basic stuff." Pointing out Sondheim's precision and attention to detail, Prince remarks, "I was able to put that number in without changing one bit of staging."

In general, he attempts to answer as many questions during pre-production as possible; the flexibility with which to develop a show *during* the process has been drastically reduced in recent decades. Directors simply cannot throw out costumes, sets, and whole acts with the ease they did earlier in the century. This is due not entirely to economics, although that is certainly a consideration, but also "because musicals have gotten more intricate, more ambitious, more integrated, and on the whole, more sophisticated. What you ought to do is go into rehearsal thinking you have most of the questions answered. You never have them all answered. And there are always some grisly surprises, but those surprises more often now require a new number, a different scene, the readjustment of a character (which is writing), but not new scenery, new costumes, and a whole new second act."

Prince takes a strong hand in leading his productions. He believes that the problem with most musicals "is the absence of a [directorial] concept. A unifying umbrella." The "concept" keeps collaborators, designers, and performers all moving in the same direction and takes the production from paper to stage. That concept, he contends, starts in pre-production. Where many directors put the emphasis of a show on casting or the rehearsal period, Prince puts equal weight on the entire process. "Tyrone Guthrie said, 'seventy-five percent of directing is casting.' You know what? That's too easy. Each of these periods is utterly important: getting the script and music right, getting the design right, casting it right. And then making contact with the actors [rehearsals]. It's just that the five weeks [of rehearsals] is a hell of a lot shorter time than all this other stuff."

When it comes to casting, Prince states, "I'm told by actors that I have a reputation of being kind and well-mannered, and I sure as hell hope so because the whole business of auditions is grisly." He admits that he is likely to hire from a pool of performers he already knows when casting a straight play, or even casting second and third companies of musicals. But when it comes to casting a large-scale musical for the first time he knows of no other way but the "uncivilized" process of auditioning. The process itself is brief; Prince rarely sees any one performer for more than five minutes. He looks for "what every other director I've known looks for" in an audition: truth. "It's really a very simple (complicated, but simple) straightforward, truthful experience that one's looking for." He does not look for a complex interpretation, believing that a performer hurts their audition if that interpretation does not coincide with the writer's or the director's. "I expect them to stand there and be truthful"; and he believes that the more props and chairs and "stuff" a performer requires to do their audition, the less persuasive they are.

The audition is a type of performance itself, unlike any other. Sometimes, Prince admits, a director can be "misled by an artful audition," and end up casting the wrong person for the role. Other times, talented actors go unnoticed, because it is very difficult to spot talent in an actor who does not know how to audition properly. These problems are inherent in the audition process itself. If he could, Prince would do away with auditions altogether, but "I wouldn't know an alternative. I can't say that I think they're civilized, but what else are you supposed to do?" One of the tricks of casting a large musical, he says, is "putting together a company of the most experienced, refined, and talented actors [with] somebody who just got out of school five minutes ago." When they are together on stage, "it's supposed to look like they're in the same show. And a good director has to make those things merge."

Prince meticulously casts his shows and then utilizes actors' inherent talent to bring life to the characters. This can be seen in the wide variety of interpretations by different actors playing the same role. "Mandy Patinkin [as Che in *Evita*] was a very different deal from David Essex who opened it in London. David Essex was much gentler, more recessive. Mandy was a punch in the jaw, good for New York." Although different, both performances worked, says Prince, but not every musical allows for such diverse interpretations; some performances, such as Angela Lansbury's as Mrs. Lovett in *Sweeney Todd*, are "definitive." But, "a simple fact of direction is that you cannot make somebody do something they don't want to do." It is for that reason that he casts actors who are similar to the characters they portray.

In the course of his career Prince has directed traditional book musicals (*She Loves Me*), concept musicals (*Company, Follies*), and epic musicals (*Sweeney Todd, Phantom of the Opera*)—all extremely different in their manner of storytelling. Yet he approached directing them all in the same way. For him, the method in which he directs a musical does not change according to the material. Additionally, he directs plays and musicals similarly. This leads him to confess that "some of the plays I've done (i.e., *The Visit*) have almost seemed like musicals without scores. *The Great God Brown*, an early O'Neill play—there's a musical without a score." But Prince prefers the musical form over others: "Once you get all those components in there, you miss them when they're not there."

His style as a director has continued to change and grow throughout his career. He admits that his early pre-production work on *Cabaret* followed the traditions of the musical theatre at that time. However, following a summer vacation to Russia where he took in a performance of *Ten Days that Shook the World* at the Tagonka Theatre, his entire understanding of theatre was redefined. "It was theatrically stunning. All sorts of styles collided on the stage in one evening. And I thought, 'Oh My God! This is the theatre!'" When he returned home he took what had been done to that point with *Cabaret* and completely reconceived it. He intentionally "splintered it," taking the character of the Emcee (a role written specifically for friend Joel Grey to represent all that was the spirit of the Berlin cabaret of the '20s and early '30s) and fragmenting his single twelve-minute number into several songs throughout the show, thus making them serve as commentary on the era and the action of the play. He further divided the play into segments of realism and nonrealism, climaxing in the "Cabaret" number in which the character of Sally Bowles metaphorically "crossed from the real world into the nightmare world of the cabaret." Nowadays, beyond the concept-musical era of the '70s, this approach to the musical theatre is commonplace, but in 1966 it was revolutionary. And it shot

Prince from the ordinary director of such book musicals as *She Loves Me, Baker Street* (1965), and *It's a Bird, It's a Plane, It's Superman* (1966) into the forefront as leader of the concept-musical era. "*Cabaret* was an expression of me as a director, as opposed to anyone else." Because of that, it changed the form of musicals.

"In the theatre the compact between the audience and the stage is an active one as it is nowhere else." Prince sees the audiences' participation in the experience as vital. "You fill in the scenery. I don't give you wallpaper. I give you a black enamel wall and a piece of furniture in front of it. You'll put in the wallpaper." An audience that has to work a bit throughout the experience is an audience that is more dedicated to it. "Everybody's looking at the stage and seeing something slightly different. And that's good. Because the more committed you are to the experience as an audience member, the more involved you are." Some obstacles detrimental to that relationship, he says, are to extravagant sound systems that make an audience sit back, rather than lean in, larger visual images, and his belief that people have shorter attention spans requiring "explosions in their faces." There are exceptions, of course, but Prince believes they are rare.

His understanding of the audience runs deep. He believes an audience needs to have "a sense that these people know what they're doing," and points out that if the company (and the director in particular) have not done their homework, the audience can sense it. Prince uses an example from *Follies* as the epitome of an audience trusting the director's work: "*Follies* had almost no scenery until the 'Follies' segment, which was the last fifteen or twenty percent of the show. I had an empty stage. It all took place in a theatre, at a party. And Alexis Smith had to sing ["Could I Leave You"] to her husband who was besotted and sleeping somewhere on this empty stage. So, she said, 'What am I doing, Hal?' [Prince:] 'Well, you're walking from upstage left to downstage right, and you're really in the basement of the theatre and there are dressing rooms on either side. And you're opening the doors looking for Ben. And suddenly you hear snoring. You push open a door, and sleeping in the most undignified, hopeless way on top of six or eight mattresses is Ben Stone. And you go in and confront him.' Now, you're in the audience; did she walk down opening doors? No. She just walked from here to here. But in her head she knew where she was walking. You, the audience, knew it was abstract, as you knew everything else up to then had been abstract, but you had the confidence to know that the director and the star knew where they were. They weren't just meandering on an empty stage. And if they had been, you wouldn't have bought the moment." The key here is "specificity. They [the audience] don't have to know, they just have to know *we* know." A director who is always aware of the audience remains true to the material.

He is not only open to actors' suggestions (and will incorporate them, "if I think it washes") but he also relies on his actors to fill in the gaps of their performance and make a consistent character throughout the work. He finds this important in the lead roles and in the chorus as well, where performers are usually left to their own imaginations. Prince states, "For years and years and years in the theatre everybody in the chorus had a character they played . . . you'd read your program: mailman, milkman, housewife, dog walker, and so on." Modern musicals, however, more often include nondescript choruses in the fashion of operetta, making the director's job more difficult. To solve this problem: "If I can, I take the whole chorus and make them one character." Then he relies upon his performers to create individuals within that structure. Such was the case in *Sweeney Todd*. Prince gathered his chorus into a "clump" and moved them about the stage en masse, a practice that seemed to generate a tremendous energy within the group. Then, within this single character (the "clump"), he challenged each of them to be distinctive by suggesting they "look in the mirror" and create a unique character within the realm of each performer's possibilities (i.e., an eighteen-year-old actor should portray an eighteen-year-old character and not attempt a sixty-eight-year-old man). Following this proclamation to the chorus, "I came in Monday and a girl was dragging her foot. And I said, 'What is that?' She said, 'It's an iron brace that they used to wear when they were paralyzed in one leg to keep them standing.' Well, we got her the iron brace and she wore it." Consequently, "It was worn by all the other people who ever played that role in the show."

Prince spends the first week of a five-week rehearsal schedule for a musical having the company learn the music and begin the choreography. "The second week I come in and we have a reading—one reading—and then we get on our feet and go." Although he acknowledges the importance of how and why and where, he will often tell his casts: "Let's not do too much talking. I can answer all your questions. I've spent the last three to five years working on these [characters]. I do not want to talk to you about the next generation, because you're in this generation. I *will* talk to you about your antecedents (insofar as the past impacts on why you are the way you are) but only to a limited degree. Let's deal with *now*."

When it comes to staging, Prince avoids the kind of pre- or paper blocking he did on his first show (*The Matchmaker*), which he admits he did because he was fearful of not appearing prepared and organized. However, he soon found that being too rigidly devoted to a set of plans left little room for improvement. "When you do that [preblock] then one very good actor says, 'But what if I went *there*.' And the whole house of cards tumbles in front of you because this actor chose to go left instead of right. And all your pre-blocking is worthless." Instead, "I don't even think about blocking." Due to his extended preproduction work prior to rehearsals, Prince will "know that material pretty damn well" by the time rehearsals begin and thus will have an understanding of how the show should be staged, even without concrete, written directions. "What I will do is, the night before I rehearse a scene I read it to myself one more time before I go to sleep." He suggests that the details of the blocking are worked out in his subconscious while he sleeps, then "I get up and go in and stage it." He blocks his shows quickly and rarely makes drastic changes during rehearsals. "There are directors who work a kind of rough-draft blocking, and then they go back weeks later and fine-tune everything. I have found only by observing that I seem to do all the detail work right away. And add to it [during rehearsals], of course. But I don't have a lot of restaging to do. The first blocking usually *is* the blocking."

He enjoys staging his own musical numbers but will turn it over to a choreographer if it requires counts. "I can't do counts," he says, referring to not just "steps" but anywhere precise movement to music must take place. He is also quick to acknowledge the tremendous contribution a choreographer can add to a show. By understanding fully the director's goals, a choreographer is capable of enhancing or even adding an entire dimension to the work.

When directing opera, Prince finds more often than not, "you're not the first person to direct these opera singers in this material. They've all done other productions. And the other productions are, more than likely, a bit more conventional." Opera performers are conditioned to arrive a few days before the dress rehearsal and "expect to just throw in the performance they did for Franco Zefferelli or someone else." Not so in a Harold Prince opera, however. "I learned very quickly that the best way to avoid having them tell you, 'This is the way I did it before,' and going to the same place they went to before, [is to] make the scenery so individual that it double-crosses them." For Prince's Chicago Lyric Opera production of *Madame Butterfly*, for instance, he replaced the usual setting (an interior) with a little house and a bonsai garden. All of a sudden "they've got a mountain to climb, a house to go into, gardens to walk around. Nothing they can do about it. They're stuck. Now they've got to do your production." Because they are familiar with the material prior to rehearsals, most opera singers can make the adjustment. "If they're smart, and good actors, like Placido [Domingo], they do it very quickly. And have fun doing it. But there are lazier examples of the breed out there who are not as good, and they really resent you."

Previewing a show can happen in a variety of ways: with out-of-town tryouts leading to New York; previews on Broadway prior to opening; or moving a show that has enjoyed an extended run in other cities to New York. Prince has used all of those methods and does not prefer one system to another. He suggests that the trend to open shows in other large metropolitan cities such as London, Toronto, or Los Angeles allows for some advantages. In particular, there is the benefit of an out-of-town tryout without the pressure to move the show into New York too quickly, perhaps before the show is ready. His revival of *Show Boat*, for example, played a year in Toronto before moving to New York, during which time "we did some good, healthy toying with it. A year later we opened on Broadway. It was a much better show than the one that opened in Canada." For *Kiss of the Spider Woman*, a show prematurely (and negatively) reviewed during its developmental tryout production, Prince and producer Garth Drabinsky took the show to Canada for revamping. Following that, "I said, 'You cannot bring that show to New York. They [the critics] will not forget that they hated it. They've got to stick with their early guns. Let's get the Evening Standard Award in London, then they'll rethink it.' That's exactly what happened. They played for six months in Canada, six months in London. I changed it a little each time. Then we came to New York. Whammo! The best." The show won the Tony and the New York Drama Critics Circle Awards for best musical of the year in 1993. However a show previews, whether on Broadway, out of town, or in another country, Prince sees the development a musical makes during those early months as invaluable.

Prince has produced (or co-produced) twelve of the more than twenty Broadway musicals he has directed. He points out that being one's own producer has its advantages. It allows him, for instance, to be the final decision-maker across the boards without having to "go through anyone." He believes this aids in bringing about a consistent production. However, he prefers not having to produce his shows. A producer of quality can be an invaluable asset, and he points to Garth Drabinsky, with whom he has done several productions, as an example. "I think he's a very creative producer. And maybe he'll nudge me once in a while to do more than I would do if I was left up to my own devices." Having produced himself, Prince knows firsthand the value of a good producer.

The regional theatre system in America is not one of the developmental institutions in which Prince prefers to create his new works, though he has tried his hand at it with *Roza* (1987). The production played at Baltimore's Center Stage and the Mark Taper Forum in Los Angeles before making its way to Broadway. "Too much regional theatre is self-congratulatory. And guess what's happened? It has hobbled a movement that was enormous. They have not come through with the promise that they had twenty-five years ago, because they haven't criticized themselves enough. I've walked too often into regional theatres and had everybody say, 'This is better than they ever did it on Broadway,'" to which he takes umbrage. "Broadway's taken an awful lot of lumps. Sometimes absolutely deserved. But the best of Broadway has often been the best there is. We just don't get it often enough."

After opening, Prince's job is not over. "I go back all the time, because no one ever did for me when I was the producer. I used to just *beg* the directors to go back and look at the shows. George Abbott, he'd go and stand behind the stage manager for about ten minutes," which for Prince is not nearly enough. He regularly sits out front with a pad and pencil and takes notes on his productions. "And then I rehearse them." Whether it has been playing for five months or five years, Prince habitually rehearses all of his productions. As the director, he also oversees and approves lead cast replacements. When a replacement is put in, "the stage manager does the dirty work but I come in, give them the first rehearsals to get them on the right track, and then see them as soon as they go on."

For Prince, the most important quality to have as a director is taste. He also believes this is important for actors and producers as well. It is taste that dictates the decisions he makes. In addition, "You have to be disciplined. You have to be educated. Some directors aren't. I think it's too damn bad. They've cut down a lot on their wherewithal to communicate. Experience, inquisitiveness, curiosity, and a generosity of spirit. All those things seem unbelievably important to me. It isn't just one thing, it's a big package. And then there's luck." Interestingly, when Prince suggests a director should be educated, he is not necessarily talking about higher education. He points to numerous examples of top-notch performers and designers who were not encouraged (and oftentimes *dis*couraged) in the college and university system. "No one's saying you can't learn from these places but don't endow them with too much." Prince believes the theatre itself is the best teacher, particularly for a young director. "There's a great deal of craft involved in directing, there's equally a great deal of courage and imagination. I think the surest way to learn how to direct is to apprentice yourself, or work for someone you respect. You don't have to become that person, you just have to learn how that person became that person. And then take your own path." Practical experience was and continues to be Prince's greatest teacher.

What keeps him going on a daily basis is his love for the work. "I enjoy working. I enjoy directing. I enjoy texts. I enjoy the company of actors. I enjoy collaboration. I don't wallow around in the pain of the last set of bad reviews and the early closing, I just move on." Prince is proud of his accomplishments, although perhaps more proud of his growth as an artist. "I also enjoy that I've put in all these years and know more now than I knew before. I think I know as much as anybody about the empty space and how to energize it. And that's a nice thing to know. Way back when I directed *She Loves Me*, I knew the results I wanted, but I had no craft and no experience." Today Prince's craft is well-honed; his end results often imitated.

Jerome Robbins

Jerome Robbins (1918–1998) began his professional career as a ballet and chorus dancer in the late-'30s. Through the ballet, he developed into a highly sought after choreographer, and put his talent to use on the Broadway stage in such musicals as *On the Town* (1945; based on his earlier ballet *Fancy Free*), *High Button Shoes* (1947), *Call Me Madam* (1950), and *The King and I* (1951), among others. Robbins is best known, however, for directing and choreographing some of the most important and highly successful musicals of the century, including *Look Ma,*

All quotes are taken from a personal interview conducted by the author with Mr. Robbins.

I'm Dancing! (1948; co-directed with George Abbott), *The Pajama Game* (1954; co-directed with Abbott), *Peter Pan* (1954), *Bells Are Ringing* (1956; co-choreographed with Bob Fosse), *West Side Story* (1957; co-choreographed with Peter Gennaro), *Gypsy* (1959), *Fiddler on the Roof* (1964), and his own retrospective *Jerome Robbins' Broadway* (1989; co-directed with Grover Dale). He was also one of the most successful "show doctors" the musical theatre has had, aiding, among others, *Wonderful Town* (1953), *Silk Stockings* (1955), *Funny Girl* (1964), and most notably *A Funny Thing Happened on the Way to the Forum* (1962) for which he supplied, with Stephen Sondheim's help, the opening number, "Comedy Tonight."

This accomplished choreographer and director, who split his career between the ballet and the musical theatre, never set out to become a Broadway director; his goal was to simply keep working. Following a brief college career at New York University, Robbins dropped out in order to become a dancer. Dancing jobs led to choreography assignments, which eventually led him to directing. What he learned about directing came almost entirely through observing others. "I was in four Broadway shows, just in the chorus but I got to hang around and watch what they did there. I had all that background [*before* I began choreographing]." Most influential, however, was his work with director George Abbott. "I did about five shows with George Abbott. Some of them I co-directed with him, and some of them I just choreographed. Now, think about that. George Abbott." Robbins believed that being able to work alongside Abbott, the renowned master of his time, was the best education he could have received. Although he saw Abbott as rather "businesslike" in his approach, he also observed "he was very fair-minded too," allowing collaborators their say even if it differed from his own. Abbott's instinct for editing (be it the script, the score, or the dances) impressed Robbins the most, for often "he was very right. He had a good mind, a very good mind." This would leave a lasting impression on Robbins and indeed become one of Robbins's own strengths. "I liked the way Abbott worked. I didn't appreciate it as much at the time as I did after a little while." Robbins would continue to work with Abbott early in his career even after it was apparent he could work independently, because, as he said, "I could learn things from him." Other influences on Robbins during his career included the work of Stanislavsky, though he never considered himself "a Stanislavsky director," and the teachings of Stella Adler with whom he studied for a time. These latter influences brought about a depth to his work as a director, as well as a more fully integrated and highly developed communication through his choreography.

Robbins saw that his ability to read music, even to a limited degree, helped him in his work in the musical theatre and particularly in the ballet, because it contributed to better communication between himself and his musical collaborators. His experience as a professional performer, however, did not appear to him to be of great benefit when working with his own performers, nor did he see that as a prerequisite for a director of musicals.

Later in his career, Robbins chose his projects very carefully and believed that his selectivity accounted for a bit of his success. He thought directors should be discriminating in the projects they take on, selecting only works for which they have an affinity; in order to direct a show effectively, he said, "I think you should like the material. Even if you hate it, you must like it at the same time. There must be something about it that makes you want to do it." Robbins was offered many more shows than the relatively few he actually ended up directing, and admitted there were a number of shows he *should* have directed but turned down. This was often due to his lack of confidence in the material for one reason or another. Though recognizing that these shows were still in their early developmental stages, he conceded he often had an inability to free himself of his early takes on the material, preventing him from envisioning a better finished product. Robbins remained reluctant to return to Broadway later in his career (*Jerome Robbins' Broadway* being the one exception) for he felt the musical theatre had lost its heart and soul and had become a showplace for spectacle: "Show me a show I want to do. Show me a show that's *about* something, that has got some gut feeling about it. I think a lot of those shows [nowadays] get along on their glamour."

He well understood how his style as a director changed and evolved over the course of his career. There is a distinct split between his early musical comedies (*The Pajama Game, Peter Pan,* and *Bells Are Ringing*) and his later, more serious masterworks (*West Side Story, Gypsy,* and *Fiddler on the Roof*). "I think I got more into it as I was going along. At first I was just putting on the scenes. Then as I studied, as I went on further, I found ways of getting things out of people that I wanted to get out of them," actors, writers, and composers alike.

As he developed, he began to incorporate a great deal of research and a number of rehearsal techniques into his productions. He began research for a show long before rehearsals commenced, usually while the piece was still being written. "I just start, and keep going and keep going and keep going. Anything that comes along, I use it," if it furthers the story or makes the piece more authentic for the audience. "If you can use it, fine," he stated, but do not use it if it does not contribute anything to the overall work. This constant exposure to relevant material built up a warehouse of ideas, which he could then later draw upon throughout the course of the production. His attention to detail through research became quite evident during rehearsals for *West Side Story*. During that show, cast members were encouraged to engage in their own firsthand research by associating with and studying actual New York City gang members and their culture in order to bring realism to their characterizations. Additionally, articles of gang activity were often posted backstage for cast members to read during the course of the show's run.

This intense research was coupled with a variety of rehearsal techniques. One of those techniques was the use of improvisation, not so much as a means to develop dialogue, but as a means to more fully develop characterization. During *Fiddler on the Roof* rehearsals, for example, he pitted cast members against one another in scenarios involving World War II concentration camp prisoners versus prison guards, and southern blacks versus white shop owners. Both improvisations were an attempt to give cast members a personal understanding of minority persecution, which they could then transfer to the plight of the villagers of Anatevka. He found the use of improvisation to be an extremely beneficial tool, though he used it judiciously; "Only when I couldn't get some point a certain way. Then we'd try an improvisation to see if that would help them."

Robbins would personally take on the task of being the final editor of the script, score, and design elements of the shows he directed: "I think the director should have the final say [in those matters]." He believed the collaborators "all should be working toward the same end, toward the same goals," and that it was the director who set those goals for the creative team, not the writer, the composer, or the producer. "If the producer doesn't agree with it, he shouldn't have that director." In his later productions he involved himself with even the minutest of details in an effort to create a fully integrated, consistent, and unified work. For this reason, he preferred to be associated with a musical from its inception (though his early career did not entirely follow this pattern), for he felt it gave him more control over the structure of the show. "I like to start with a show from the beginning, which means you're also writing it at the same time and helping develop it." For *West Side Story*, *Gypsy*, and *Fiddler on the Roof*, "I was around while they were being written, and so I had input there." Having the director on board from the start, he believed, makes the shows stronger and more unified—not just on the stage, but on the page as well. For Robbins, this collaboration made the difference. It gave him a stake in those shows unlike some of his earlier musical comedies: *"Bells Are Ringing* anyone could have done." He believed that to just direct a musical would be "very hard" and much preferred his role as both director and choreographer: "That way it gave me a little more ability to hang stuff together." His example and success would usher in the era of the director-choreographer as a major creative force in the twentieth-century American musical theatre, paving the way for other renowned greats such as Michael Kidd, Bob Fosse, Gower Champion, and Michael Bennett.

He saw the collaborative process as stimulating, even though he admitted it could often be frustrating simultaneously. During the long gestation of *West Side Story*, for instance, he said, "I'd try to get the guys together [Leonard Bernstein, composer, and Arthur Laurents, author] and couldn't. They didn't want to do it! Then they came back to me several months later and said they had another project they wanted me to try out [a musicalization of James M. Cain's novel *Serenade*]. I looked at it and said, 'No, I don't want to do that.'" Another hiatus followed. Months later in Los Angeles, Bernstein and Laurents would stumble upon the format their *Romeo and Juliet* would take (Puerto Ricans versus "Americans," rather than the original idea of Catholics versus Jews), and took it to Robbins. Excited by the new premise, he took the helm, and *West Side Story* finally moved into the writing stage— literally years after the idea was first born. Another collaborative headache for Robbins was *Peter Pan*, which was originally produced by Edwin Lester on the West Coast for his Los Angeles and San Francisco Civic Light Opera Associations. The show had a score by Moose Charlap and Carolyn Leigh (music and lyrics, respectively), about which Robbins did not feel confident. Being unable to collaborate with the original writers, he brought in favorites Jule Styne, Betty Comden, and Adolph Green to augment the score before the show made its way to New York. The musical's libretto, "which was based on a conception

I took from the book" went through a number of revisions (and writers) as well, leaving Robbins, out of necessity, to "help write the whole thing." In the opening night Playbill, however, the book remained uncredited.

As a collaborator, he stressed realism and plausibility in the structure of his shows: "I don't like to add stuff that helps get a song in if it doesn't fit in the show." And because he was on board from the beginning, he was able to integrate dance more fully into the storytelling of his later shows. The contribution of his dances in *West Side Story*, for example, do more than further the plot, they also help define and develop the characters "because some of the action went on *into* the dance." The key lies in getting into "the psyche" of the character, "which is what the dancing is. Dancing is what they're feeling, and what they want to do, and how they want to do it. It has to be, if you want it to come out strong." This was the approach he took in 1957 when the show first appeared; he concluded, deservingly, "I was really so far ahead of myself in doing *West Side Story*." Evidence to support his claim appeared almost forty years later when the New York City Ballet's repertory revived the musical's dances under the title *West Side Story Suite*: "I did a whole half-hour or thirty-five-minute piece of dancing which I took right out of the show. It's a big success. Audiences love it. I am surprised. For the thing to be just as successful, the dances being just as vital, and everything working just as well is still a little bit of a shock to me." Robbins was quick to point out, however, that like songs, dances must come from the story itself and that each show will dictate its own movement. "You can't put certain kinds of dances in certain kinds of shows. It just doesn't work." His use of show-specific dance was clear throughout his career, perhaps nowhere better illustrated than in his integrated use of ethnic dance in *Fiddler on the Roof*. Robbins believed that dance was not as often integrated into the musical theatre of the '70s, '80s, and '90s, not because there were fewer director-choreographers producing integrated work (although that is true), but because writers were not writing dance into their musicals. "They don't write it. The writer doesn't write 'that certain thing happens in the dance' which changes the story. It doesn't happen in *words*; it happens in the *action*." The concept musical of the '70s, for example, often replaced action on stage with narration, thus eliminating the need for choreography to help further the story.

Ironically, though he spent a great deal more of his career working in the ballet than on the Broadway musical stage, he concluded that ballet itself can only be of limited benefit in the musical theatre. "Ballet work is just a technique, a way of dancing certain roles. If you get good dancers in the musical theatre who can do all the ballet things, then you can get them to do almost anything. If you can get them to do *only* that stuff then you're stuck."

For Robbins, one of the most important jobs the director performs is casting. "You wake up to a lot of surprises if you cast incorrectly." He believed a good deal of his success was directly tied to his casting choices. He admitted that on occasion he cast the wrong person, but rarely was it ever so detrimental to a show that he had to replace the actor. "If you think you can get out of them what you want, you stick with them. If you can't, if you think you're not getting out of them what you need, then you replace them. Thankfully, I haven't had much of that problem." He enjoyed the audition process, even though he conceded that assembling the sixty-two-person cast for *Jerome Robbins' Broadway* was a chore. "That was a hard show to cast because of the variety of things that everyone had to play. And they had to switch from role to role as they went from scene to scene." And although he often worked with big-name stars in his shows (Mary Martin in *Peter Pan*, Ethel Merman in *Gypsy*, Zero Mostel in *Fiddler on the Roof*), he suggested that not every show requires or is written appropriately for a star. Such was the case with *West Side Story*, for which he cast an ensemble of young, unknown talents, thus suggesting that a director must examine the show's needs before simply engaging a name for the name itself. Regarding *Gypsy*, he said, "Mama Rose was a wonderful role for Merman. It was written for her in mind. But Gypsy herself [Sandra Church] was an unknown. She hadn't done anything before. It depends on the part. It depends on how big the show is, or *what* the show is." In general, he tried to cast individuals who were innately similar to the character they played. "How's it going to come out with her playing it? You can't make her [the actress *or* the character] into something she's not." Once a director has an understanding of the character, they should then have an understanding of the performer appropriate for the role. "Once you sense that that person can play the character then you start thinking of the character in her terms."

Although Robbins began his professional career as a dancer (and then choreographer) he did not feel he put undue importance on dance ability over other areas during his auditions. He was careful to keep the individual show in perspective on its own terms first and foremost. For instance, he had originally wanted dance to play a greater role in *Gypsy* than it eventually did. But once Ethel Merman was signed on as Mama, Robbins's take on the show adjusted accordingly; Merman was not a dancer. "She didn't have to dance too much in *Gypsy*, but she could jig around a little bit and she did that. She had a good sense of music and humor." Since she was brought on board while the show was still being written, the creative team (including the director) could tailor the show to her strengths, thus Robbins's dance show took a backseat to Merman's talents as singer and comedienne. Most often, however, actors are auditioned and hired after the show is written, as was the case with *West Side Story*. Even with this dance-heavy show, Robbins cast a variety of performers with a wide range of experience. "I was looking for people who could do both [act and dance], and fit in anywhere. I didn't need classic dancers. I needed some, and I got some." Some of the "authentic juvenile delinquents" he selected had no dance experience at all, and he waited until rehearsals began before he determined exactly how he would use each performer in the show: "We didn't know if that guy was going to be a dancer or what [when we cast him]. If he couldn't dance a step we didn't put him in any of the dancing." Overall, he cast the show appropriate to the characters on the page, and not on dance ability alone.

Robbins acknowledged that he was a dictatorial director ("that's a fair assessment") but he said he never asked more from others than he was willing to give himself and he never saw anything wrong with being demanding, believing it brought out a person's best work. Although critics have often cited him as being extreme in his dictator-like approach, one must balance that opinion against the results he produced on stage. Robbins justified his work ethic by suggesting that "a single piece of art is wrought by a single vision." He believed that vision should begin with the director. "He should have his eye on everything. It may seem to take care of itself very nicely, and may not need any more comment on it. But you may see someone missing something completely," and in that case, Robbins believed, the director must step in immediately before any harm to the overall work is done. To insure that all the pieces of the puzzle come together, one often has to boldly put forth a single vision to which the company can adhere.

This strict work ethic was not necessarily evident early in his career when at times, he confessed, he began rehearsals for shows before the script and score were even complete. Later in his career, with the structure of the libretto being so vitally important to him, he preferred to wait rather than go into rehearsals, until the writers had a completed (or mostly completed) show. There were times when "the composer was still working on a song, or a couple of songs he had in mind," at the time the show went into rehearsal, but in general the shows were whole. "Mostly I've had it happen that you write new material while you're out of town working—an 'out-of-town song' it's called." He believed that a good number of "out-of-town songs" were some of the best pieces written for a show. He attributed this to the depth of understanding the collaborators had developed about the show and with each other by that point in the process. "You may come up with a great idea, and you may not. But usually they're good songs because by then they [the composer, lyricist, and author] are functioning correctly. We're all functioning, we hope, correctly by then."

The rehearsal period for Robbins was sacred, and he detested being rushed through the process, as exemplified by his often unprecedented work schedules. *West Side Story*, for example, had an eight-week rehearsal period at a time when most other musicals were given four or five. "We had a lot of work to do, and I was starting from scratch: new score and new music." *Jerome Robbins' Broadway*, a show for which Robbins felt he needed the cast members in front of him in order to recreate musical numbers from a career spanning more than forty years, had an unprecedented twenty-two weeks of rehearsal. "You read about how in Japan and London and other places they take time and time and time just to work it out. I prefer that to our three-and-a-half weeks, two-and-a-half weeks, four-and-a-half weeks; getting it all done and having it all ready and putting it on." Because of that, Robbins was an advocate of regional theatres, which give shows a first production prior to Broadway. "I think that helps," he said. "Anything that gives you time helps."

He preferred his casts to have done some homework on the show by the time rehearsals began. "I don't like them to discover the script the first time they look at it at the first rehearsal. That's a little late for me. I like it when they come in and they know what they're talking about, and they know the script quite well." He acknowledged, "Some people work better at finding it during rehearsals, searching around for it, playing around with it," which he deemed acceptable, but "when I get into the second or third week, they better start knowing what they're saying."

The opening number of a show was particularly important to Robbins. He saw this to be crucial in establishing the parameters and rules under which the evening would unfold. For *West Side Story* the opening confrontation between the Sharks and the Jets told through ballet not only established an immediate conflict between rival gangs (which ultimately led to the climax of the musical) but also announced that dance would be instrumental in telling the story. *Fiddler on the Roof's* opening number also told the audience the basis upon which the evening's conflict would hinge: tradition. "We thought that up after my probing around and pushing around at it. Saying, 'What the hell's this show about?' And thinking and thinking about it. And then finally saying, 'it's about a tradition.' The guy gets three chances to change. He changes on two of them, but on the third one he can't—he can't give up the tradition. And the whole thing breaks apart." Robbins's metaphor of the instability of life ("as shaky as a fiddler on the roof") was established in the opening minutes and subsequently woven throughout the entire work.

Robbins had no "formula" for directing, no specific approach he followed for every production, since he believed that the rules changed with every show. "I think it depends on the musical, it depends on the play. Each play presents you with a different problem. Otherwise, it would be a bore. Directing *Oh Dad, Poor Dad* [*Mama's Hung You in the Closet and I'm Feeling So Sad*; one of the rare straight plays he directed] and directing *Fiddler on the Roof* were two different problems," and thus could not be solved similarly. Once in rehearsals, he would slowly and meticulously work his way through the show from beginning to end, tackling each problem as it arose. "I would just start on the first scene, see how far we got, and then see what happens. You just go in and work it out," again not rushing the process and begetting mistakes. Robbins did not pre-block his shows, nor did he pre-choreograph the dances or ballets within those shows. Although he approached rehearsals with a strong physical sense of how the show should look, he believed theoretical preparation was inadequate and preferred working out the specifics of the staging in the rehearsal hall. "I *can't* work it out ahead of time. How can I work out what thirty people are going to do without having them there in front of me?" Though he did not necessarily invite suggestions from his cast members, he noted, "They usually speak up if they have ideas—if they're good ideas." At the beginning of blocking rehearsals he liked to "show them the set and where the things are. An actor, if he's good, like Zero [Mostel] or someone like that, they pick up on everything. You can't put a shoe box down on stage without him using it somehow." Believing it is the director's responsibility "to get the most out of the script," Robbins would often try a scene several different ways, not stopping until he achieved the right look and interpretation he was seeking.

When it came to characterization, he did not leave the actor's interpretation to chance. Here again he would clearly (often through staging, movement, or direct line readings) delineate to his performers how he wanted particular roles performed. "I believe that we all have the same conception of the characters and how they want to be used by the script." With that, Robbins strove to bring out that single interpretation in his actors. He saw the process as a transference of power from director to actor; taking the director's interpretation (actually the omnipresent interpretation existing in the script, which the director knows more comprehensively at the outset) and transferring that understanding to the actors. "You get into it slowly and easily, and then the more they get used to the part, the more they get used to what the character is like. Then you've got them going." Once this understanding is transferred, the actor can then flesh out the character in ways consistent with the dictates of the script. Though he agreed that the characters take shape around the original cast members, he did not rewrite scripts to perfectly fit his casts. Illuminating the script remained the goal for the actors. If he had had other actors, then their approach to the material might be slightly different, but the goal and the interpretation would remain the same.

He confessed that he held the reins on his actors rather tightly: "I don't let them do what they want. I'd like them to have some *version* of what I'm after. I don't say that my answers are always the best ones, or the only ones, but they're the only ones I can come up with." Sometimes, however, actors refused his guidance. In such cases, Robbins advised, "You have to take a look at it. You have to let them do the scene the way they feel they want to do it and see how it fits into the whole scheme of the show. If you feel it really breaks it then you have to get them to switch around if you can." During rehearsals for Arthur Kopit's *Oh Dad, Poor Dad* he encountered such a conflict with the show's original Madam Rosepettle, played by Jo Van Fleet. At the first read-through, "she read one of the scenes just brilliantly." He thought to himself, "'Well, I don't have to worry about that right now. I can hold onto that scene. That's only a two-person scene. I'll wait on that.' And I got to it and she didn't do anything like it. She said, 'Oh no, I don't want to do that.' I said, 'Well, how come? You were so brilliant. You had me laughing on the floor. I couldn't ask for anything better.' She said, 'No, I think I better try it a different way.' I could see she didn't want to do it my way. She had something in mind—I don't know what it was." Eventually, Robbins acquiesced: "As long as it worked I said 'Alright.'"

Though he directed only two straight plays (*Oh Dad, Poor Dad* and Brecht's *Mother Courage and Her Children*) he approached directing them in the same fashion as he did musicals, though perhaps with less conviction about his vision. "I did one show that I should not have done and that was *Mother Courage*. I don't think I was prepared for that. I suspected it [heading into rehearsals] and it turned out to be true." Because he was "unprepared," it left him open and vulnerable to other people's interpretations and suggestions. "I had about five hundred teachers. Everyone had their own idea about how it should go. And I listened to everybody. I didn't enjoy that show."

Once a show opened, Robbins felt it was important for a director to check back on it from time to time, although he admitted it was a task he loathed. "I don't like to, but I'll drop in quite often to see how it's going or if I want to check on something. I don't like to go see it again and again and again." He prefers instead "to keep a good stage manager there who's watching it carefully." He did like, however, to oversee cast replacements "if they're important ones," but preferred not to go back into rehearsals once a show was up and running "unless they've had so many new people in it that it needed some rehearsals."

Robbins's approach to revivals of his own work was considerably different than the way in which he mounted his original productions. (He never directed a revival of a show for which he was not the original director.) For the 1980 Broadway revival of *West Side Story*, for example, Robbins worked much more quickly for his questions as a director had already been answered previously: "It was finished now, so I could go right to it directly. I didn't have to spend days trying stuff and seeing whether it worked or not." He would simply remount, rather than reinterpret, the original production, which he knew worked. Interestingly, he believed shows should be reexamined and reinterpreted by *other* directors and artists.

Robbins saw the new desire and economic need to give shows multi-year runs as detrimental to the theatre. "The whole course of show business has changed. Now the idea is to do a big, big show that will run for many, many years and stay put. The length of a show's run is getting longer and longer and longer. So, that show stays that way, and it isn't redone." An additional problem with extended runs is that shows may evolve and move away from their original intent and direction. "I don't think shows should have long runs. They [the actors] get bored with them. How are they going to make it fresh for three years?

They can't tell when it clearly slips away from them. It would be nice if we could have fresh people in there all the time." According to Robbins, part of the problem stems from the new way in which musicals are produced. "Producers aren't what they used to be. They're just not. You used to have people like Leland Hayward, George Abbott . . . I remember them keeping their distance, and letting me go. [If they had a suggestion,] they'd come to me and say 'You know, I think this thing is somewhat this way or that way.' But they'd bring it up with me personally." He felt producers of the '80s and '90s were far less interested in the *show* and more interested in the *business*. "Now producers are interested in the money aspect of it. They're interested in raising the dough, keeping the dough going, getting the dough coming in, and making the deals on everything."

Robbins also acquired a good deal of experience working with children in productions such as *Gypsy* and *The King and I.* Although he admitted "it depends on the kids" whether they are easy or difficult to work with, he found that as long as they understood what was being asked of them, "they react pretty well. There's no secret to working with kids. They either charm you and you can work with them, or they don't charm you and you feel you're stuck with them." He treated the children he worked with just as he did the adult actors and believed that may have been a fundamentally good decision on his part, though not a conscious one at the time.

Ironically, for as much time and energy as Robbins put toward research and long intricate rehearsal periods on his own productions, he had perhaps more success than anyone in the latter half of the century working as a show doctor on other director's productions—a job that required him to work in complete contradiction to his style as a director. Here he was often asked to observe an ailing show, recognize trouble spots, and create solutions to problems with limited time, resources, and possibilities. Often, he suggested, the solutions lay in pointing out obvious mistakes that the creative team no longer recognized as problematic. "If you can see things that are just disastrously wrong—obvious things—then you try to fix them." Such was the case with *A Funny Thing Happened on the Way to the Forum*: "That was someone not thinking deeply enough about what they were doing. It started out with sort of a nice ballad, 'Love Is in the Air.' And then very slowly the humor started to work in. I said, 'I think that's all wrong and I think it is for this reason: you've got to tell the audience what this show is about. You've got to make them understand this is a comedy. Let them get used to the fun of it. They're ready. They'll laugh at anything. And then you'll be on the right track.' So, they did that, and it worked. Then the whole show began to switch." Again, laying importance on the opening number, Robbins had the subtle "Love Is in the Air" replaced with the more comically raucous "Comedy Tonight." His staging of the number was so unique that it warranted inclusion twenty-seven years later in his revue *Jerome Robbins' Broadway*.

Overall, Robbins was most proud of his work on *West Side Story* and *Fiddler on the Roof*, not because of their impact on the genre, their success, or their integrated use of dance within the structure of the stories they told, but because "both are about minorities, and that made them worth doing." Robbins did not necessarily see his career path as one that might be emulated by other directors wanting to succeed in the musical theatre. "Each director has to figure it out for themselves. I'm sure there are many, many ways. There can be complete opposite ways from what *I'm* doing. And still, if the guy has a good head and is after certain, exact things it will come out all right." Above all else, he believed a director must know one thing as he or she heads into any project: "What's it about? What is the subject to you?" By having a personal, in-depth understanding of the show on its own terms, and through research and a rehearsal period in which one continually strives to find *the* interpretation, not merely *an* interpretation, a director of quality will emerge.

George C. Wolfe

George C. Wolfe first found success as a writer with his plays *The Colored Museum* and *Spunk*, before emerging as the director of such musicals as *Jelly's Last Jam* (1992; for which he also supplied the book), *Bring in 'da Noise/Bring in 'da Funk* (1996; for which he received a Tony Award), and the 1998 Broadway revival of *On the Town*. Wolfe's numerous Broadway credits include Shakespeare, contemporary dramas, musicals, and both parts of Tony Kushner's Pulitzer Prize–winning *Angels in America*.

All quotes are taken from personal interviews conducted by the author with Mr. Wolfe.

Wolfe initially entered Pomona College in California as an actor and designer but soon focused on directing and writing. ("So, by the time I left college I had sort of done all the disciplines.") Following college he worked in Los Angeles and then New York teaching and holding various theatre jobs before entering New York University's musical theatre program as a book writer. "I didn't go to NYU to learn anything; I went to NYU to buy time so I could be an artist full-time and write full-time [and] to make a connection with various artists, with various professionals who were working. And that happened." He points to such professionals as book writer Peter Stone, director-writer Arthur Laurents, and director-lyricist Richard Maltby Jr., as being particularly helpful in getting him "into the room" where people could see his work. "I like to break rules a lot. Each of them in their very specific ways taught me a lot of rules. And not just the rules, but understanding the rules—which is very important. Because if you break the rules without knowing them then you just create a mess. If you break the rules and you know them, chances are you can create something that's innovative." Although learning the rules is important to him, he sees them as merely technical, intellectual applications. "Anybody can learn rules. What makes you unique is your voice. A lot of times when people learn the rules first it takes them a long time to find their voice. With having the rules under your belt you maybe work sooner, or figure out how to function within the system quicker, but in retrospect, I was very glad to do it my way because when I arrived, I arrived with my voice intact."

Particular *moments* in the theatre, rather than other directors or artists, have been the most influential factors in the development of Wolfe's directorial voice. "'The Quintet' from *West Side Story* was very liberating for my brain. The 'Bowler Hat' number from *Pacific Overtures*; the way that was staged and written by Hal [Prince] and Steve [Sondheim] was crucial." For Wolfe these were doorways of information, which allowed him to pass through to another level of thinking. "Sometimes the smartest thing you can do for an artist is to show them a doorway. Not necessarily to show them what's inside the room, and not necessarily to tell them what to do once they get inside the room, but just to show them a doorway."

Although he holds an M.F.A., he does not see the university system as effective in training young directors—"not in any way, shape or form"—and suggests that the best way to learn directing is simply by directing. "I question anyone's aspiration to become a Broadway director. I think it's a foolish thing to aspire to. I think what you should aspire to do is to become a *director*, and work as many different places as you possibly can. I think you should do the classics, I think you should do new work, I think you should do musicals. I think you should try to do it all. That's not to say that you're going to do it all *well*, but cultivate all these different muscles, because the different areas end up feeding each other." Some directors learn by assisting others and he suggests this as a possible route for burgeoning directors, although not one which interested him. His education came through "listening to smart people talk about theatre. Not *talented* people necessarily, because oftentimes talented people are not smart [at] talking about what they do. So, you always want to find very smart people who talk about theatre."

He also believes a director (particularly of a musical) should be well versed in all areas of production: "I think a director needs to do as many different jobs in the theatre as is possible. I think it would be good for a director to act, I think it would be good for a director to design. . . . So he has a sophisticated vocabulary when he's talking to all of these creative people, as opposed to just saying, 'Do it because I say to do it.' If you can make somebody see your vision, and incorporate their vision into your vision, you end up getting eighty times more passionate, intense, and committed work than if you just sort of put a vise grip on people. If you know how to speak their language, and you have certain skills in each of those areas, then I think it provides another kind of link for the collaboration."

Although he saw the musical theatre as a rather closed "club," particularly to artists of color, he was persistent in his desire to be accepted. "I had been around for a very long time doing work—doing smart work, doing good work—[but] once I was able to make those connections I could get into the room." Getting into the room, however, was not getting into the club, but merely a plateau where he could demonstrate his ability. "*Jelly's Last Jam* [his first Broadway musical] did not get me in the club. I think it was *Angels in America* before I was let into the club. I think it was *Angels in America* simply because it was the first project that I had done up to that point that was not directly about African American culture."

He sees an unfortunate division in America between black musical theatre and white musical theatre, which he believes is perpetuated and reinforced often in "unconscious and subliminal" ways. He points to Martin Gottfried's pictorial history of the musical theatre, *Broadway Musicals* (published in 1979), as just one example. "Since the very beginning, black people have been involved in musical theatre. Some would say that the minstrel show is the grandparent of the Broadway musical. [But] no black people are mentioned in the entire book until at the *end* of the book—or at the back of the bus, if you will. All the black musicals are clumped together in one chapter. So, you turn one page and there's *Shuffle Along* [1921], and you turn another page and there's *Ain't Misbehavin'* [1978], and you turn another page and there's *The Wiz* [1975]."

He believes the key ingredient new artists of any race need most in order to compete and "join the club" is opportunity, and as producer of the Joseph Papp Public Theatre in New York, he works diligently to provide those opportunities. "The thing which I've been able to do is invite artists into the room. Invite as many different kinds of artists into the room as I possibly can. I just keep on trying to introduce new talent. Not just black talent, but all kinds of people. The thing that you can most do is empower any artist to feel as though they have a right to go on the journey. I'm in the club now, no doubt about it." Because of that he feels an obligation and an opportunity to bring others in as well.

When choosing his projects, Wolfe favors shows he feels "deeply, rawly passionate about. I don't know why to do it otherwise." However, that is not the only criteria. He does not shy away from works that appear difficult; in fact he prefers them: "I choose projects if either they scare me, or I don't know how to do them, or there's some landscape to the piece that I'm really interested in exploring." There are lessons to be learned on every project, even if their true value is not obvious at the outset. This was the case when Wolfe was presented with the opportunity to write the book for a new musical entitled *Mr. Jelly Lord* (later retitled *Jelly's Last Jam*). Though he was not initially passionate about the project, the offer lingered for many months. "Clearly the fact that it wasn't going away was a signal to me that there was something in there that I needed to pursue." He eventually agreed to the undertaking. "Then at one point I figured out *why* I had to do the project: that this was an important journey for me, a personal journey for me. But it was three years into the project before I found out!"

With the Duke Ellington musical *Queenie Pie*, another show for which he supplied the book, the lessons he learned had little to do with play production and more to do with the business of theatre. He sounds a warning to young artists: "In a first meeting people [producers] say to you, 'Hi, I'm going to screw you.' They announce it to you. And if you're so busy being in love [with the project] or being so desperate [to work, then] you don't hear it. *Jelly's Last Jam* taught me things about myself: it taught me cultural things, musical theatre things, Broadway things. I learned all sorts of active career stuff. Whereas *Queenie Pie* taught me lessons on how to be smart in the business."

Wolfe likes to be on board a project from the start. "As a director I'm a conceptualist. I don't just stage things. One of the fun things to me is conceiving the conception of a musical. How it works, how it's put together, how the ideas bounce off of that." What excites Wolfe about the genre is using the different elements inherent in the musical theatre in unique and varying combinations. "It such a whore form; it steals from everything. It takes singing from opera, it takes dance from ballet, it takes language from straight plays. My theory is: if you have a weapon, use it. And in the musical theatre you have all kinds of weapons. You should use the whole realm."

Dance is a favorite weapon of his. The shows *Jelly's Last Jam* and *Bring in 'da Noise/Bring in 'da Funk*, for instance, were built around dancers. "I think that music and dance have a purity to them that spoken words don't have. I think it's a much more subliminal form of communication. Language pricks the brain, whereas I think music can affect us on such primal, unconscious levels." It is that type of subliminal, thought-provoking, emotion-filled communication that Wolfe brings to his brand of musical theatre. "What I hate most about musical theatre is just mindless giddiness. I can't tolerate it, unless it's flawlessly, brilliantly done. Something like the movie version of *Singin' in the Rain* is so flawlessly, brilliantly giddy that it creates another kind of euphoria inside of you. But a lot of musicals don't."

Wolfe's directing approach remains the same regardless of the genre. "Maybe other people direct musicals and plays and classical work differently, but I don't. I think there are different muscles that you use, but I think intellectually and craftwise it's very similar." The task for him is to take a script and then figure out how to infuse it with an energy that makes the work urgent. "The difference is, every single thing that you're doing fundamentally in a musical is defined by a meter, and a very specific meter. In a play it's also defined by meter, but the meter is crafted by your understanding of the play, and the emotions and the intentions of what the actors bring to the table."

He approaches musical revivals in a similar fashion as he does original musicals, although with one slight difference: "I'm trying to figure out how to make it a new play. I hate revivals that feel like they have a coating of campiness and nostalgia." He recognizes that different eras produced different styles of musicals, although he contends that the goal of making the work immediate remains the same. "Any work of art is in theory connected to real emotions. Now, the *style* that it may choose to release itself in can be farcical, can be campy, can be anything. But you always try to access the reality of the situation." When, for example, a colleague suggested to Wolfe that *On the Town* appeared written like a cartoon, Wolfe disagreed. "It didn't seem like a cartoon to me. Madam Dilly is not a cartoon of a music teacher, she's a very real person who, because her career didn't happen the way that she wanted, has an exaggerated sense of her own significance." Though the character, the situation, or the show itself may seem larger-than-life, Wolfe keeps his revivals firmly rooted in reality by "perpetually looking for the truth. I've seen a bunch of shows that have been done where it's just sort of like this grotesque manifestation of comic behavior that has a slight hint of humanness attached to it. I really find that exhausting and not pleasant to be around."

Wolfe believes that the writers of a work should turn over the final editorial chore to the director. However, as a writer himself, he admits he would be reluctant to do so with his own material unless working with a director for whom he held great respect and trust. Eliciting the trust of his own writers then is a key goal for Wolfe when directing. "I'm a ferocious collaborator. And I don't think I pull any trips or any games or any of that power crap, but if I don't believe it, I'm not going to do it. If somebody can make me believe something, or can convince me, or help me understand something, then I can do it." Although he believes his instincts are good and that he can recognize when an aspect of the show is not working, that alone is not enough for him. "I then want to figure out *why*." Probing into exactly why something is not working, through constant and open discussions, reinforces the choices the collaborators make by demanding the team justify their decisions. Oftentimes, in the midst of these discussions, better choices come to light.

Sometimes he works without a script at all. Such was the case with *Bring in 'da Noise/Bring in 'da Funk*. The entire show was created during a three-month period beginning with a three-week workshop in August 1997. At the end of these three weeks the company had forty-five minutes worth of material. A two-week hiatus was followed by a second set of rehearsals beginning in September, which led directly into previews the first week of November. "It was just a phenomenal collaborative period," benefited greatly by the fact that "everybody in the room had worked with everybody. So we had already evolved a vocabulary." Though he loved working improvisationally, and the show proved to be highly successful, he does not anticipate creating a great many more musicals in that manner: "We were very blessed that that experience turned out as glorious as it did, [but] you don't want to tempt the fates too much."

Wolfe views pre-production work—evolving the vision of the piece with the writers and designers, and casting the show—as the most important work the director of a musical performs. It is the foundation upon which everything else rests. Poor decisions in a show's development or sloppy execution during this time can ultimately undermine the entire production. Of special interest to him are the designs of the show. "[The director must] evolve a visual vocabulary with the designers that doesn't necessarily solve the entire play, but gives you all the visual tools you need to solve the play." He spends a good deal of time working with the designers: "But not just in designing the show, but [in] coming up with enough flexibility in the design, so that as you start working on the piece and as your vision evolves, the design can adjust to that. A lot of times people come up with a design and then they're slaves to that design . . . and that's deadly." He contends this has never happened to him and explains that his early career experience as a designer helps him anticipate design problems before they arise.

In auditions "spirit and a sense of their own magic" are just as important to Wolfe as an actor's talent; these are the qualities that make the talented performer stand out from the rest. "You cannot act those [qualities], you have to have those." Talent, however, is by no means ignored, and Wolfe is apt to seek out "really smart actors who can sing really well." Furthermore, he notes that directors must be aware that not all actors have the versatility to be successful in all styles of musical theatre. He believes a lot of actors performing in the present epic-musical era have lost (or never obtained) the broader acting style of earlier musical comedies. "There are people—talented people—who are completely and totally wrong for *On the Town*. Really talented people, but they were not able to throw themselves inside the silly intelligence of that piece." Additionally, the epic musical ("this pop-opera of *Les Miz* and *Miss Saigon*") has decreased the actor's responsibility to find and act the emotional truth of a moment, says Wolfe, for emotional content is often linked directly to the music that accompanies it. "It really doesn't matter what he [the actor] brings to the role as long as he's singing the big ballad that has [pseudo-]emotion attached to it—but doesn't have to be really emotional. They can do the voices but there's no real emotion going on. What ends up happening is they become machinelike."

He points out that the audition process is often a lengthy one, but necessary if a director is to ensure an ensemble of quality. With *Jelly's Last Jam*, for example, it took six months of audtioning before he was satisfied, "simply because with a lot of black musicals the work doesn't require the gut. [Early black musicals] required 'energy' and 'vitality' and a fake kind of sex appeal. But nothing really edgy, and nothing really dangerous. *Jelly's Last Jam* required an attitude and a sexuality and a presence and a dynamic that I don't think is often asked of black artists in the musical theatre. Particularly in all-black shows."

He acknowledges that a big-name star's reputation can enhance the draw to a show and benefit the box office, but his main reason for bringing a star on board deals more with their ability to tell the story than sell tickets. "Gregory [Hines, who led *Jelly's Last Jam* in the title role of Jelly Roll Morton] understands intellectually and instinctively how to invite an audience into his world. And when you're dealing with a character like Jelly Roll Morton who, as we were exploring him, had a lot of negative components to his personality, it was very important that I have somebody in that role that could completely and totally invite an audience into the process. A lot of actors are so busy working that you can't get inside. Stars fundamentally know how to let an audience in. They create room for you to go inside. That's the real brilliance of a star."

Wolfe does not think in terms of "miscasting" roles, nor does he feel that any of his performers have led to the demise of a production, although he admits that there are times when an actor's role develops beyond one's means. "You cast people, and maybe they're perfect for where the production is at that point in time, [but] you realize that your vision or the work has evolved in a different direction." It is for that reason Wolfe prefers to mount his shows more than once. "The first time you do a piece you *learn* it. The second time you do it I think you can evolve it to the next level. If I thought [casting] changes were necessary, I made those changes when it moved. It's not because the people are not talented enough, or there was a mistake made in casting, but your vision of the role evolved."

He sees himself as both dictatorial and permissive in his approach to directing: dictatorial in holding to his vision; permissive in allowing others to contribute to it. Prior to rehearsals he does quite a bit of research to build up a reservoir of information about the piece, the period, and the characters. From this he comes up with "certain abstract ideas of what I want, certain 'connect-the-dots' that are not connected." Then, as he heads into the rehearsal process with the actors, he allows them to contribute freely to his vision. He admits that he is, to a certain degree, dependent upon the actors' input to fully flesh out the production. "One of the fundamental rules of musicals is it needs to have a unified vision, and I think I'm really good at unifying visions, asserting mine and incorporating other people's into that vision." The key to consolidating all those visions and motivating his actors to do their best work lies in his philosophy of collaboration. "I think there are two fundamental schools of directing: either you stand where you are and demand that people come to you, or you go to where people are and woo them in the direction that you want them to go. I think it's ultimately eighty times more exhausting but more fulfilling to go to them and woo them. And sometimes in the process of wooing them, they woo you. I believe that if you go into a project knowing everything, what you end up doing is recycling old truths. And that's how work ends up stale. Therefore, you have to go into a project and allow yourself to *not* know, which is the first step in discovering new truths."

When directing a straight play, Wolfe spends a good deal of time during the first week of the rehearsal process sitting around the table with the actors talking, reading the script, "and analyzing what's going on underneath almost every single line." Then they begin to "play around with it." He approaches musicals with the same intense attention to analysis, although he delays the initial read-through of the show until later in the process. Instead, he begins by showing the set model to the cast, talking generally of ideas he has for the show, and sharing any research materials he has obtained that he feels pertain in some way to the show and his interpretation of it. Following this the company immediately gets to work learning the music, the songs, and the dances.

"Then maybe at the end of the first week we have a sing-though/read-through . . . so that the people can sing a bunch of the stuff and put it all together. So the first time you read it they're aware of the shifts of rhythm that happen with music and language . . . [making] them aware of their responsibility to the rhythm of the whole."

At times during that first week he may work individually with people on particular scenes to get them thinking about certain dynamics he has discovered in the text. Often he will ask specific questions of his actors—questions concerning characterization, motivations, and the like. All of this is intended to stimulate the actors to question the material for themselves. Once the company has "dismantled" any preconceived notions they have about the material, then they can view the text without limitations. Wolfe believes this dismantling is stifled if decisions are made too quickly in the process, or blocking commences too early. "If you start doing work too soon everybody's recycling some shit that they figured out on the last project they did." Forcing actors up onto their feet before a thorough analysis of the script is completed can be detrimental later in the process. "[If you block too early] you're blocking what you *think* it is, but you don't *know* what it is yet. I use the rehearsal period so I can *learn* what it is, so we can learn together." The time the company spends planting these initial seeds of the production is invaluable, and he avoids rushing the process. "Anything you skip, you pay for later. If you skip over the discovery process, you pay for it later. If you skip over learning time, you pay for it. I did *The Caucasian Chalk Circle* and [at the first rehearsal] we had a read-through around the table. Then the next day I came in, the table was gone, and they all went, 'Where's the table?' And I said, 'We're blocking,' because I was reacting from my own insecurity, and I wanted to stage the whole thing. And I think until the final week of performances those actors always felt insecure, because I took away the table too soon." He also uses that first week as a time for the company to get to know one another. Not until sometime during the second week of rehearsals does he begin to stage portions of the show.

He has no interest in pre-blocking his shows ahead of time ("that's boring"). Instead, "I let them play and then shape it, and sometimes impose it. I don't put things in form for a very long time. Some actors need it right away and so I try to do a little version of that [if necessary]. Other times I just let it play for a while, and see how it evolves. And sometimes the evolution is good, sometimes it's not good. I think it varies on the kind of actor that you're working with. I always say, if push comes to shove—if we're in previews and it's not working—I can block this scene in ten minutes. I can put it in a really solid form. But let's come up with a form so people can continue to play. Make it as rich as you possibly can. You don't have to seal something too soon. Because, once again, it can suffocate the energy, and you end up having to go back and redo it."

He also executes a good deal of the musical staging in his shows and works closely with his choreographers to create a seamlessness in the show's movement. He prefers not to "rigidly define territory" between job descriptions, admitting, "I invade everybody's territory. You know, I come up with an idea, I give it to somebody, they ride with it. Or they come up with something . . . " This interaction allows the creative team to best serve the entire production and not limit itself to (or become territorial over) individual aspects of the show. However, to ensure continuity, Wolfe requires all the information and ideas to be funneled through the director.

He recognizes that the actors' growth during rehearsals is often a slow and difficult process. "You've got to allow actors to make mistakes in the rehearsal process. You can't just demand that they be good all the time, because if you demand that they be good all the time they're going to wait until performances to start making mistakes. There is a rhythm and there's a dynamic to the rehearsal period and you've got to honor that." Because of this, he prefers the writers not be present at rehearsals. "I think the actors have got to be able to make a mess of the material, and they're less likely to make a mess if the person who created it is sitting in the room." (Ironically, he does not find this to be a problem when directing a show on which he is also a writer.) The actor's growth, Wolfe notes, does not happen overnight, and he is careful to educate the company in his vision before turning the show over to them. "You can always tell when an actor is smart enough to talk about the material. I don't mean *intelligence*, I mean they're inside the material enough. If somebody starts saying the first week, 'I don't like that line.' You just go, 'I'm not listening to a word you say because you don't know enough yet.' Now, after about two weeks (if you're a really smart actor), maybe after about three weeks, or probably more likely when you're in previews and you're living with the material, I will listen to you in a whole other way. [As a director] you have to gauge who's saying it. Is it a smart actor? Is it the smartest part of the actor's brain? Is it actor's ego? Is it actor's fear? You have to listen because every actor has different people who talk."

He feels the same way about producers in the rehearsal hall as he does writers. "I'm not a fan of creative producers. I don't think it's a good thing for them to hang around on a regular basis. Come in and see the work at a certain point—two weeks of work is done, come in and see it. I do a run-through, come in and see it. That's fine. But every day? No. Comments about this song or that song as you happen to walk by a room and hear it sung, I'm not interested." A lot of shows have more producers than cast members; in such instances, though he still allows them their say, Wolfe puts restrictions on how he works with the producers. "On *Angels in America* there were [he exaggerates] 857 producers and I said, 'I will talk to *one*. So, you all talk to each other, narrow it down, and then I will be glad to have those conversations with that one person.'" This way of working proved to be beneficial for all concerned.

The preview period is a very important time for him, and he uses these performances as a sounding board for what works and what does not. He takes what he learns in previews and immediately applies it in daytime rehearsals, which keep going concurrently. Actors benefit as well, "because actors now have knowledge that they bring in; not just knowledge of their craft, but knowledge about the play. They've seen what works with audiences." Wolfe looks upon previews as a "fun time to work on the show," despite the fact that fine-tuning a piece on Broadway is "oftentimes very painful" as well. "*Jelly's Last Jam* was a painful process because it significantly changed when it was in previews. And it's always so painful doing anything in New York City." In general, the process requires the director to walk a fine line. "I think the truly difficult thing about directing musicals [is] being available to everything without becoming distracted by everything, particularly in a high-pressure preview situation. When you're working on any piece of theatre, the signals come from every single direction, and you've got to be ready to hear them or see them. You can't be so available to everybody that you're wishy-washy, and you can't be so rigid that you don't receive information when people are giving it to you. I think, in many respects, that's the true craft of directing—aside from knowing how to move people around and all that. [It's] being smart and focused and tough and available at the exact same time."

One aspect of the director's duties that Wolfe dislikes is maintaining a show after it has opened. "To be perfectly honest, I really hate that . . . something about it feels painful going back and living where you've lived." Despite that, he, his stage managers, and his assistants continue to monitor each production whether in New York or on tour. He confesses that some shows maintain themselves better than others: "It depends on who the stage manager is [and] it depends on how disciplined the cast is." Regardless, he believes it is important to check in on a show and give notes when necessary. "I'd say for the first year there's a very specific thing that happens, because there are very specific rhythms. And then after that my presence becomes less frequent."

Those different "rhythms," or phases, a production naturally goes through that first year affect how it needs to be maintained. "It's like dough. By the time the show opens the dough is sitting in the pan. And then after a while it starts to rise. What you have to do is . . . figure out how it can grow in the right way and not grow in *every* way." For the first "few months," Wolfe believes a show goes through a healthy development in which the actors "begin to add subtleties and depth and complexities" based on their growing insight of the show and their roles. During this time Wolfe acts as a gardener for the actors "pruning things that have grown that are not necessary, and making way for other things that have grown that weren't initially there by the time you opened." Throughout this process (the first three to six months of a show's run) he is also educating his company, "cultivating inside the actors their own editing machine" so they eventually become the checks and balances of their own performances. By the time the show has been running nine months "certain rhythms of excitement and boredom" begin to alternate with one another. During this time he often begins to see unproductive experimentation creep into a show. "Where that first period of inventiveness generally is a very, very smart inventive period, after about nine months 'inventive for the sake of being inventive' can start to color a prcduction; at which point in time you just have to step in and do some editing out. Generally, after about a year the actors are very, very smart about it, and can gauge when it's on. Then you can step in infrequently, or an assistant can step in, and just tweak it and fix it periodically."

Wolfe will often retain say over cast replacements, although "it depends on the nature of the project" as to whether or not he will rehearse the replacement actor into the show. "Generally what will happen is a stage manager will put a person into the show—they'll do the blocking, they'll have them work with actors, et cetera—then when it comes time for a 'put-in' rehearsal, I'll be there and then give them notes afterwards. Then for the first couple of performances I'll check in and out to see how they're doing." This varies with the complexities of each production. For *Angels in America*, "I did extensive rehearsals prior to them even going and working with the stage manager." He is conscious about letting replacement actors bring their own abilities to a show, but notes that there are more restrictions put on them than the original cast members: "You have to allow them to bring their own stamp to the piece. At the same time you also have to protect the show."

Overall, Wolfe believes a director should not try to approach each musical in the exact same way. Each show's unique qualities must be recognized and developed if old truths are to be dismantled and innovative material allowed to be innovative. "You have to find what is immediate in the material, what is urgent in the material, and then invite your collaborators, the actors, and the audience into that process. That's what you do. In that order. Then everybody feels as though they're connected to something that's important or that's immediate or that matters. And when you can access that it's exciting."

Jerry Zaks

After making a name for himself as a successful play director (primarily with comedies such as *The Foreigner*, *Lend Me a Tenor*, *Six Degrees of Separation*, and a number of Christopher Durang works including *Sister Mary Ignatius Explains It All for You* and *The Marriage of Bette and Boo*), Jerry Zaks directed his first musical in 1985 when he was asked to mount the national touring production of *The Tap Dance Kid* (1984; directed on Broadway by Vivian Matalon). Since then he has directed a number of musicals, including *Assassins* (1990),

All quotes are taken from personal interviews conducted by the author with Mr. Zaks.

Smokey Joe's Cafe (1995), *The Civil War* (1999), and three highly suc-
cessful Broadway revivals: Cole Porter's *Anything Goes* (1987); Frank
Loesser's *Guys and Dolls* (1992); and Stephen Sondheim's *A Funny
Thing Happened on the Way to the Forum* (1996).

After completing his M.F.A. at Smith College, Zaks came to New York
in the fall of 1969 determined to be an actor. He worked regularly for
ten years appearing on and Off Broadway in plays as well as such musicals as *Grease* (1972), *The 1940s Radio Hour* (1979), and *Tintypes*
(1980). All the while he had "no interest in directing whatsoever." Then
an old college friend suggested Zaks direct him in a low-budget, four-
performance production of the Neil Cuthbert farce *The Soft Touch*.
"And I said, 'Why not.' It was really sort of serendipitous." At the time,
"I was totally unfamiliar with the joy of directing, or the satisfaction that
directing can give you." But as he stood in the back of the theatre watching those performances unfold, "I fell in love with the theatre all over
again. The joy that I experienced in watching what I had shaped with
the actors, and then refining it and trying to make it better, ignited me."

Zaks refers to himself as "a musical comedy illiterate. I think that's
one of my strengths. I'm the opposite of someone who grew up loving
the Broadway musical. I wasn't aware of it until I got to college." This,
he suggests, accounts for his success in mounting revivals. "A lot of
these [old musicals] come to me and I read them as new pieces. I go,
'Whoa! *Guys and Dolls*! This is great!' There's no reason it couldn't
have been written yesterday." Although he does not feel obligated to
simply reproduce the original production when approaching a revival,
he does not ignore a show's history either; on the contrary, he uses it
as a template from which to learn and create. "I do my research. I'm
aware of their former lives. I use the preexisting shows as springboards
for my own invention."

Some of the shows Zaks chooses to revive contain inherent greatness, yet he will not shy away from creating his own if he feels it to be

just as valid. "With a new piece you have no answers. With a piece that's been done, depending upon what kind of record there is of it, you have answers but you don't know if you want them. You don't know if you like them. And in some cases they're so impressive, you don't know if you can do better." That was the case with "Comedy Tonight" in the opening of *A Funny Thing Happened on the Way to the Forum*. "Jerry Robbins's version of that is legendary." Zaks debated, "Do we want to ask Jerry Robbins to come in and redo the opening and maybe make it even better than he did? Or do we want to come up with a different version of it?" He had a couple of ideas of his own which, if integrated, would not coexist with the Robbins's version; and while interviewing choreographers, he found himself more drawn to those who suggested a fresh interpretation. In the end, he abandoned the safe approach (the Robbins version) in favor of his own.

He does not, however, believe it wise to change aspects of a show merely for the effect of doing it differently. Inherent in a number of shows are aspects of the storytelling that cannot be changed without disrupting the rhythm and makeup of the show itself, and Zaks is careful to recognize these traits before deciding upon a different path. A case in point is *Guys and Dolls*. "When Tony Walton [scenic designer] and I first sat down and started considering ways to present it scenically, we investigated ways that would allow us to present the show in something other than a series of alternating in-one, full-stage, in-one, full-stage scenes." This is a practice often employed in midcentury musicals in which a short scene is presented downstage before a drop ("in-one") while the larger set for the next, longer scene, is being placed upstage of it. Following the short in-one scene, the drop flies out and the action continues directly into the larger, "full-stage" scene. Shows such as *Guys and Dolls* (1950), *South Pacific* (1949), and *The Sound of Music* (1959), for example, were written specifically to utilize this convention. "Any attempt we came up with to create a multipurposeful space to avoid bringing a drop in I was afraid would compromise something in the inherent rhythm of what was written. The scenes that were 'in-one,' if they were done on a full stage, would seem lost; there was an intimacy to those scenes that allowed them to happen in-one. And then [there was] a size to the 'full-stage' scenes that demanded that they happen on an open stage. So, we learned from the original what we'd probably better not try to do for the sake of being different."

Zaks does not believe intelligence alone is enough for a director when approaching a musical; they must also have a "nonintellectual" response to the material. When he was presented with the script of *The Soft Touch*, for example, "I read the play and it made me laugh out loud. And in fact, that's really the barometer I use now as much as anything as to deciding what I'm going to commit to. Unless the material elicits from you some sort of ecstatic response when you read it in anticipation of creating that kind of ecstatic response in an audience, it's not going to happen. Unless you have that response I don't think you should direct it." For him, it is "*essential*" that the director likes the material he or she chooses to direct. "You can't underscore it enough. You must remember, I was an actor. I regarded [directing] as an avocation, and so I was very picky [about the projects I took on]. I wasn't desperate to direct. I think I was desperate to act. And as an actor I accepted things, and it didn't matter how I felt about the material as long as it gave me an opportunity to perform. It's a different kettle of fish as a director. You must fall in love. Otherwise, when it gets tough, and it *will* get tough, the need to do it will not be strong enough to sustain you through the process."

Zaks does not read music, though he acknowledges that the ability to do so would benefit him when directing a musical. "The more things you know, the better you'll be. My anti-intellectual sort of point of view does not preclude the need to know as much as possible about everything that you're doing." For this reason, he sees the university system as a fine starting place to learn, practice, and prepare oneself for the professional theatre. He believes young directors can "get experience in working with musicals in the better theatre schools—in the undergraduate programs that have musical theatre programs." And while he does not see graduate M.F.A. programs as necessary for success, he does recognize that his own graduate program helped him tremendously. "The university is your playground to build up a head of steam. It's critically important, because you will get knocked down eventually [in the real world]." Beyond the universities he believes "getting involved with a musical on some level, [even] as a production assistant, just to observe and watch the process in action is useful." Ultimately, however, "there's nothing like having the responsibility for doing it yourself." Zaks himself learned through "trial and error" and does not rule that out as a possible path for others. "My advice to anyone contemplating directing musicals is: direct plays first. It starts with you and a group of actors and a script. Start slowly. Learn as you go. Equip yourself with the tools."

Directing suits his personality: "By nature I like control," he says. Because of that, he classifies himself as rather dictatorial in his approach to directing. "You have to understand that when I'm talking about dictatorial I'm talking about insisting on acting choices that serve the storytelling. So, I have to structure things to allow actors to feel free and safe to invent. But there's self-indulgent invention, and then there's invention that really serves the situation. There's invention that is simply about displaying a person's character in a vacuum, and then there's invention that has to do with that character playing the situation as though his or her life depended on it. I have to tell the difference. I make it very clear when an actor's being indulgent—as early as possible—that they can't go that way."

At the same time, he realizes that there is a fine line between a "benevolent dictator" (as he refers to himself) and a tyrant. "Hopefully,

[I'm] not so much of a dictator that anyone is inhibited from expressing themselves to me." It is here that a director can stifle their cast, and ultimately the show, if not careful. "It's not just about control . . . it's about knowing that unless I do it my way [it's not] going to be as good as it can be." From this single vision he then opens himself up to the contributions of others to make his vision a reality. "The contradiction here is that as authoritative as I might like to speak about this subject, there's no underestimating how dependent we all are on the good ideas of our collaborators. I promise you that. You can know everything there is to know about directing, [but] if you're not willing to be met halfway by your collaborators, it doesn't mean anything. So, a lot of my work has to do with eliciting the trust and the respect and the desire . . . of my collaborators to give me what I want ultimately." If he is successful in walking that fine line and in motivating his collaborators, then they invariably push themselves further than they would otherwise, and "do their best work."

In the beginning, hiring collaborators was a crap shoot for Zaks. "When you're beginning to direct musicals you don't know who is out there except by reputation to do these various jobs: to be your choreographer, to be your musical director. How do you find out? Well, you can talk to people. You can interview possible candidates. Or you can, in the process of interviewing them, see what the possible candidates bring to the table." He prefers the latter. When "auditioning" choreographers for *Guys and Dolls* he gave the candidates three specific choreographic/staging problems of the show to solve before they met. Not only did this give him a specific focus to the interview, but it also allowed him to observe how each went about their work, how prepared (or unprepared) they approached the meeting, how their two personalities meshed, and a little bit about how they interpreted the show. "When Chris Chadman [eventually hired on as choreographer] did his presentation it made me want to jump up and scream! It was fantastic!" Similar was his experience in hiring Eddie Strauss as musical director for *Anything Goes*. "He had an idea that this should be a swing band. What he brought to me was a tape that he'd prepared of different songs done by swing bands to which he hummed the melody of the *Anything Goes* score. And it was brilliant. That's how you find your collaborators." Finding a creative force with which to team yourself is only half the battle. "Then you hope that the person is not an idiot. Then you hope that the person's sane. Then you hope that the person wants to collaborate with you, and has a bedside manner, and understands how to work with people, and is willing to trust me and listen to me." If he finds they do not, "I get rid of them, because life is much too short and the process too hard."

As a play director, he notes that his comedies often had a "musicality" in their staging and "an awareness of a playwright's rhythms." This no doubt helped to inspire Norman Rothstein when he offered Zaks the opportunity to redirect *The Tap Dance Kid* for its national tour. "All of a sudden I was directing a musical, but all it meant was there were more people to talk to." The transition from play director to musical director was an easy one, for he approaches both in a similar fashion. "The only difference between a play and a musical is that there are more parts to a musical, more things for the director to concern himself or herself with. There is no mystique in directing a musical. The essential task is the same: telling a story that will transport an audience into a place that is hopefully religious." The key, he believes, lies in the acting, and he sees his experience as an actor as being extremely beneficial in this regard. "It's helped me be able to meticulously deal with acting choices. It's enabled me to understand why a scene is not working as well as it should be working; and this is plays or musicals." He contends "a director who doesn't have that [acting experience] is only half a director," though he notes there are exceptions.

He cites the films of director Elia Kazan as having the greatest influence on his work as a director. "I think he's the greatest. He understood what made it happen, and how the hell actors get to it." He feels strongly that a director of musicals should strive for solid, three-dimensional acting from their performers, and if they do not, "then that's the sure way to shitty musical theatre. If you condescend to the actors in musicals, then what you'll get are the kinds of performances that give acting in musical theatre a bad name." This desire for strong acting stems from a love of the performance. "What I love most about directing is the interaction between myself and the actors, is modulating performances, is dissecting why a scene isn't working. If it is working, how can it work better? If you accept the premise that there is no such thing as perfection, then it absolves you of ever settling. If you keep working, you can keep making it better. Just take a look at some of the musicals on the boards. Take a look at how abominable some of the acting is, and you'll understand that these people have not been directed to act."

Additionally, Zaks feels strongly that the transition from dialogue to song should neither impede an actor's ability nor allow for acting shortcuts; it is merely a heightened emotional state in the storytelling: "Any song in a good musical is a result of character. They *have* to sing. There's no choice. Emotionally words will no longer suffice." It starts with finding the "life and death stakes" propelling the action. Even in a showstopping production number such as "Sit Down You're Rocking the Boat" from *Guys and Dolls*, he does not merely approach it as a song; on the contrary, "Nicely-Nicely Johnson is faced with a cop at the door. He's got to come up with a way out, otherwise it's curtains. So he sings. And all the other guys sing with him, because if they don't they're all going to jail. That's life and death. And if it's not then the number seems gratuitous."

Zaks feels the director must act as the final editor of the script and score, but believes it should be done in consultation with the writers. "I'm going to tell them whether it's going to work or not, whether the audience is going to care or not. Now, it's all theoretical until we get into previews. So, you do as much pre-production work as possible. You pretend you've an audience in your head, [and] you imagine them laughing, or responding, or paying attention, or getting involved, or *not* getting involved and you act accordingly." He sees the book to a musical as critical to any success a show may enjoy. This is the reason he worked so diligently with writers John Weidman and Timothy Crouse to create a new book for his revival of *Anything Goes*. "The reason I did *Anything Goes* was because I was not familiar with Cole Porter's music. Someone gave me a tape of all the songs that were intended to be in *Anything Goes*, and I listened to them, and I had that reaction: 'Oh my God, these are great!' That made me want to do the show. Then I read the book and my heart sank. The joy inherent in the music is so strong that you're going to suffer some sort of a letdown when you get into the book scenes because the spoken word is not as thrilling as the song lyric. And so it puts a tremendous burden on the value of those spoken words to be important, to be smart, to be funny, to be surprising, to be passionate, to be good storytelling, and not fat, or slack, or lazy, or general. In something like *Smokey Joe's* [*Cafe*, a musical revue] where there is no book, it's really sleight of hand. It's all about juxtaposition and numbers, and changes of tone that keep the audience involved."

Though working out the details of a libretto can take some time to accomplish ("with *Anything Goes* I devoted eight to ten months, maybe even a year of work with the authors before we even began to get serious about casting"), he believes it is worth the wait, rather than entering into rehearsals while material is still being written. "With *Assassins* I think there were some songs yet to be written [when rehearsals began], but we had a pretty good idea of what the beginning, middle, and end were going to be certainly. I'll try not to do it again, because even if you think you're going into rehearsals with a completed one, there's going to be changes either in the rehearsal process or in the preview period," changes that are more difficult to evaluate properly if still in the midst of writing the show. For all of his hard work during pre-production on the *Anything Goes* script, unanticipated changes still occurred: "[At] the first preview I realized I had four openings; we started the show four times. I eliminated three of them and then we were off and rolling."

For Zaks, pre-production is a crucial time during which the director must have a thorough understanding of the show in order to facilitate its transfer from page to stage. "It's anticipating what the production's going to need. Are there fights? If there are, can I stage them? Would I be better off with a fight choreographer? Casting is a critical part of pre-production. If it's a new piece, how much script development is necessary has to be determined. Hopefully, I wouldn't have said yes to doing it if it needed much in the way of work on the script." What appears most important to him during this period, however, is "working out with my set designer how [the set is] going to work, what it's going to look like, what it's going to feel like. Is it going to establish and help a tone that you want, or is it going to get in the way of something? How is it going to be your friend and ally? Hopefully transitions have been anticipated if it's a musical [with] many scenic changes. These are a critical part of the show." Zaks tries to avoid lengthy scene changes, which he sees as detrimental to keeping the audience involved: "How will the transitions happen so that we can keep telling the story without dead time, without giving the audience a chance to sit back, space out, anticipate what's going to happen? How can we relentlessly assault them with our evening so that they're transported?" Regarding *Assassins*, he admits, "I made a mistake. I went for a set that was much too heavy and too cumbersome, and it should have been lighter and more flexible with less moving parts. The show was problematic to begin with because of its subject matter, and it was a revue, and it culminated in the assassination of Kennedy. But if I could do it over again, I'd come up with a simpler design to allow the action to flow from scene to scene a little more magically. So there's no attempt at verisimilitude. [If] it was all in some sort of limbo space in which all these crazy assassins found themselves . . . I think it would be better."

Zaks enjoys the audition process. "I like to see as many different people as possible because someone's going to come in and make me go, 'Whoa! I'm in love!' I like seeing people because—on stage, anyway— it's really hard to fake it. Some people just can't act on stage." Though he comes into auditions with strong ideas about the characters, he tries to remain open-minded to different looks and approaches. For a director of revivals, where a first impulse might be to cast according to the characteristics of the original actor and not the character on the page, this is particularly important. Zaks's casting of Walter Bobbie as Nicely-Nicely Johnson in *Guys and Dolls* is a prime example. "Nicely-Nicely, patterned after Stubby Kaye [who played the role in the original 1950 production], was meant to be heavy. And every overweight actor who came in and auditioned didn't do it for me. Then Walter Bobbie came in, who's anything but fat, and he was just great: effervescent, buoyant, and wonderful." Bobbie was ultimately cast. The choice was made early in production not to pad the actor to avoid artificiality. Zaks saw no reason why Nicely-Nicely could not be played without the weight, but the script still reflected Kaye. "If you look at the book of *Guys and Dolls* it's pretty perfect. But there's one scene that begins with Nicely-Nicely coming on stage with a bag of groceries. It was about a page scene between him and Nathan [Detroit] that wasn't working. You knew it was meant to be funny, but it wasn't getting laughs. And, oh, Walter was doing everything he could to try to make it work; he'd come in with different food hanging out of the bag, and have a different take on the scene. And I'd get frustrated because I'd think, 'Well, it's in there for a reason. Clearly it's our fault that it's not working.' And then finally I read the scene again [and realized] this was a fat joke! The only way it could really work was if the guy was clearly a glutton, which, no matter what Walter did, would never ever be." Realizing the scene contributed no necessary plot information, Zaks simply cut it from the show. "Just lifted it right out. Walter was heartbroken for a day because he felt somehow he should have been able to make it work"; but the show lacked nothing by its deletion. "And instead of having a moment that felt like he was trying to do something and failing, we just didn't have the moment."

The key to Zaks's approach in casting is recognizing the inherent needs of each character within the context of the show. "When you do certain kinds of musicals you need people who can act a song—call it 'sell a song'—a combination of sing them brilliantly and act them in a way that is totally engaging. There's certain [other] shows where all you need is a great voice and a good look, and just stay out of the way of the song. [For] certain sung-through shows, someone can appear to be the best actor in the world, but you give them lines to say and the magic goes." Ultimately, his reason for almost every decision he makes boils down to a single idea: "Whatever best serves the show. And that includes replacing people who are not fulfilling it to the degree to which they have to. And, you know, that's the hardest part."

When casting errors occur, Zaks believes that, for the sake of the show, the error must be recognized early and the person replaced. "With *Guys and Dolls* I cast a woman in the role of Sarah Brown with whom I had worked [previously], who is one of the most charming performers in the world. She was not right for the role. I didn't know that when I cast her. She moved me in the audition. We got into rehearsals and I did everything I could to try and make it right in the scenes. But some things you just can't affect as a director. When you make that kind of mistake it has a domino effect in the worst possible way. Which is to say you spend all your energy trying to improve what is essentially a mistake, and other areas get ignored. If you're good you can improve the problem by 10 percent, but it's still massively wrong. And because you've improved it ten percent you sort of feel, 'Well, alright, I'm cooking now.' Then you get into previews and that's where reality hits. Our first preview [of *Guys and Dolls*] was a disaster. The audience did not like it. I knew they didn't like it. I was dying. And I thought, 'Why don't they like it?' And there were several reasons, but of course, I was focused on the Sarah Brown situation. We went into several previews. Meanwhile, other things that should be worked on in previews were being ignored. There is a point of no return. I knew it was approaching, but we hadn't reached it yet. I still thought it was salvageable. And then a couple things happened. I heard a boo in curtain calls. I've never heard a boo in any show I've ever directed. Chilled my blood. [Following that] I pretended that I hadn't anything to do with the show, that I had paid $65 to come see it. And I watched it, and I went, 'We have to make a change.'" Once the actress was replaced, Zaks could then more easily focus on other areas of the show demanding his attention, and prepare it properly for its Broadway opening.

The structure of Zaks's rehearsal schedule from show to show remains essentially the same. "The first day the cast and the producer, everyone comes and meets and greets and it's like the first day of school." Following that, he likes everyone to stay and listen to a first read-through of the show. With the producers, designers, writers (if it is an original piece), and other personnel on hand during this "artificial performance situation," he admits, it "puts a kind of pressure on the actors that is not entirely fair but very useful to me, because I can see where they're going with their first instincts. I don't put *too* much stock in it, but I get a certain amount of information from it. Once that's done, I clear the room of everybody that has nothing to do with the actual process, everyone but the actors, the stage managers, me, and my assistants." From this point on "I don't allow people in rehearsals." Once he has the actors alone he gives them three rules to follow throughout the rehearsal process, because "getting it right is hard enough that it really can't afford to be complicated by backstage cancer. One of the keys to the longevity of a show, assuming it's a good show to begin with, is fighting that off for as long as possible. I don't think you can underestimate the value of creating an environment and a set of rules that will keep that at bay. I can't legislate people liking each other, but I can, to a certain extent, legislate behavior that allows them to respect each other somehow" and work constructively in cooperation with one another.

Those rules are: (1) "Don't be late"; Zaks abhors wasting precious rehearsal time. (2) "Don't give fellow actors notes. And by that what I mean is to not make it their business to comment in any way on what anyone else is doing, or to request anything from anyone else so as to facilitate something that you would like to try. To never put yourself in a position as an actor where you're directing. Now, if an actor has an idea about how a bit of business might work, I want to hear about it. And it doesn't preclude an actor trying something in the middle of rehearsal that we hadn't discussed, which forces the other actor to have to react, which might lead to some wonderful, unexpected moment. But if an actor has in their mind imagined something involving *another actor*, I want to hear about it [first]. So, what I'll also tell the actors is [(3)] if you have an idea, tell me in private." This is "to protect the possibility of my really listening to it properly. If you as an actor in front of twenty-five other actors say, 'Listen, what if she did this?' there's no way I cannot feel twenty-five people waiting for me to make a decision, and therefore obscuring my ability to really consider whether that's a good idea or not." To ensure a unified and consistent production, Zaks prefers to have all the information, ideas, and suggestions channeled through him, rather than have them develop independently around the rehearsal room. Beyond those few rules, Zaks tries not to interfere with the way in which each actor creates his or her role. "It doesn't matter to me how they prepare or what their technique is," as long as their performance is believable. "If I don't believe them then I'll tell them that I don't and why. Then I'll let them figure out how to get to where they are believable."

Following the initial read-through, Zaks generally likes to read and "act" the play around the table for a couple of days in order to allow the actors to get an understanding of what they are saying, and give them a chance to ask questions about aspects of the script they do not understand. Then, beginning with the opening scene, he puts the show on its feet. "Openings are very important to me. It's the first thing that happens to an audience, and they're either blown away by something wonderful, or they're just waiting. One or the other. So, you take your pick. I would suggest blowing them away in some fashion is preferable to having them just wait and watch and be politely interested." This does not have to be a loud, forceful attack; a subtle approach can be just as effective, "but it's got to make them smile. It's got to make them happy to be there." The openings for *Guys and Dolls* ("Runyonland") and *A Funny Thing Happened on the Way to the Forum* ("Comedy Tonight") have built-in appeal. What was less distinguished for Zaks when he read the script was the opening to *Anything Goes*. He needed something to catch the audience's attention. One day while listening to an old recording of Cole Porter singing the title song to his own piano accompaniment, Zaks became intrigued. "He had this tinny little, not very substantial voice. I thought, 'Wouldn't it be great if that's how the show started?' The audience is listening to this really scratchy recording, now they're drawn in, because it's small. And all of a sudden you cross-fade the recording with the orchestra. You go from 19-whenever-it-was-recorded to *now*. Well, you know, that's good; [and] the reason it's good is because it gets an audience here [pointing to his heart], not here [pointing to his head]."

Zaks consistently pre-blocks his shows on paper prior to rehearsals. "It's something I used to do by myself," but nowadays will often assign to one of his assistants "I would sit in my office or at home with the script and with the set model in front of me (or the ground plan certainly) so I knew where the furniture was, where the entrances were, etcetera. And I would pretend to be all the characters. I would note entrances, exits, crosses, sits, stands, and also work out business, work out sequences, choreograph business when appropriate. I would basically try to come up with a traffic pattern based on who was pursuing whom and why, and who wanted what from whom." By notating the blocking ahead of time, Zaks instinctively dictates each character's motivations, and through this he can communicate to his actors his interpretation of their character and the delineation of beats as he sees them. He admits this is "very limiting, [but] it's a place to begin."

Rather than simply transfer his paper blocking directly to his actors, however, Zaks likes to keep the plan to himself. He prefers to utilize the actors' creativity and instincts first in an effort to develop staging that is both natural and communicative. He allows the actors to feel their way through the scene, making obvious entrances and exits noted in the script, as well as letting them experiment on their feet. "I'll let the actors go until it's so obvious they really don't know what they're doing and then I'll make a suggestion—usually based on what I've pre-blocked— and sort of fold in my blocking when I think it's helpful. All of this is ammunition. Very often if I'm not prepared with something to fall back on, rehearsal time is wasted."

When it comes to staging musical numbers, he says, "If it involves steps then the choreographer will do it. If it doesn't then I will probably take a first crack at it. Sometimes you really don't have to move in a heightened, dancelike way to perform a song in a way that will help fulfill its role in that particular piece. [However,] I haven't seen a musical number yet that hasn't been helped by specific moves here and there from a choreographer." He prefers sharing musical numbers with the choreographer. After he has staged a number, for instance, he will often show it to the choreographer for suggestions, and vice versa.

Ultimately, he feels movement and dances must be motivated and must serve the story. When these goals are not met, it is the director's responsibility to point it out. At times, he notes, too much choreography can be detrimental to a song, and recognizing the needs and motivations within a number is key. "The audience needs to get to know the characters. The audience needs to understand what they're singing. If there's too much movement you can upstage the substance of what is happening by the style in which it's happening."

A Zaks production is often notable for its swift pace, a quality born out of a "fear of boring the audience. I'm just terrified about that. And sometimes I insist on it to a fault. But, you know, pace is really not speed, it's an illusion of speed. It's about clarity, it's about tension, it's about life-and-death stakes. It's about a desperate need to communicate something to someone else. This is Acting 101." Following each rehearsal, he likes to sit down with his assistants "if there's time and energy" and go over that day's rehearsal, evaluating the day's work and anticipating the work still to come. By the time a show goes into technical rehearsals, he notes, it is easy to lose sight of the show: "[Because you're] dealing with the set and the clothes and the props. You don't really get the piece back together again until the end of the tech process as you approach the first preview." For this reason he finds it critical to utilize rehearsal time productively.

A proper understanding of the audience—knowing how to listen to them and how to properly interpret their reaction to a show—can be crucial. Because of that, Zaks finds the preview period just as important in the development of a show as pre-production or rehearsals. "The first preview is only the next part of the process; you have to do it in front of an audience. You have to make what's only theoretical into something that's real and practical based on an audience response. Once you get into previews reality comes crashing in. And you realize what's good and what's not good because the audience tells you. You listen to the audience." In a sense, according to Zaks, at that point the audience becomes the editor and barometer against which all else is measured. He would much prefer starting previews on the road, rather than opening directly on Broadway ("Opening a show in New York, without going out of town, is barbaric."), but notes that the cost of doing so nowadays is often prohibitive. Other ways of preparing a show in front of an audience, such as through workshop, regional, and Off-Broadway productions, he finds limiting to the creative process. Regional theatres, for example, he says, have a problem attracting "first-rate people . . . unless there's a promise of the show coming into New York," and Off Broadway can rarely offer directors the opportunity to explore the script as they might need to because "everything's a bit compressed" in terms of available time.

After opening, Zaks's involvement in a production decreases dramatically. He will occasionally return to view a performance, but on the whole prefers to turn the show over to a highly competent stage manager who will keep the show in check and give notes to the actors when necessary. Hiring a quality stage manager, then, is a top priority for him. "It's a hard job: to have the authority without being officious, to be fair, to not play favorites, to have the skills to watch me in rehearsals and to absorb [my direction]. They're there every minute of rehearsal so they can see what I'm doing, they can hear what I'm doing, they can see what's important to me." Being able to absorb a director's interpretation of a show is important for a stage manager so that he or she can pass that direction back to the cast during the run. When it comes to putting in cast replacements, Zaks says, "If it's a nonfeatured part, and I'm not available because of a commitment somewhere else, I'll let a stage manager do it all. I will at the very least try and come see a run-through before that person goes on. If it's a more substantial part, then I'll try to be present. If it's Whoopi Goldberg coming in to replace Nathan Lane [in *A Funny Thing Happened on the Way to the Forum*] and she indicates a desire to work, then I will work with her as much as she wants to work. If I suspect that the experience will be life-enhancing and not life-shortening, I will dive in as much as possible."

He would rather be fired than lose creative control of his show to a producer, he says. "I defy a producer to give notes to actors in my show. I defy a producer to be seen backstage talking with an actor in a show without me knowing. I will protect what I'm doing with my life. I'm being a little melodramatic, but I don't want to understate for a second how passionate I am about the work that I do." At the same time, Zaks recognizes the producer's investment in a show: "The producer should have the right and means to express their concerns to the director when the director is ready to hear what the producer has to say. At a certain point in the process I will invite the producers in, and they will sit and watch it. Then I will go off with the producers away from everybody else and listen to what they have to say. Or, if there are ten producers, one will be assigned to represent all the producers and that producer and I will sit down and he will express his concerns to me. If they have twenty thoughts and one of them makes sense, or helps you understand something, then it's valuable to have sat with that producer and listened. When I did [*The Marriage of*] *Bette and Boo*, Joe Papp [then producer of the Public Theatre] sat me down after the first preview and had thirty notes. Three of them were great, and they went right in. That's a great percentage."

Ultimately, the director's success or failure is revealed in the audience's response. Zaks says, "When a musical begins something is launched. And once it's launched it must never be allowed to come crashing to earth. My job is to make sure that once it's aloft the spell that is hopefully being woven is never broken. [That spell] can be broken in many different ways. It can be broken by extraneous material, material that's not being performed properly, directorial overcomplication, actor overcomplication, scenic or lighting overcomplication. That's my responsibility. The audience will tell you if you have succeeded in keeping it aloft by the roar that emanates from them when the lights go down at the end. You know when you get a roar of appreciation. It's totally involuntary, totally noncerebral. That's what I want to elicit, and I can't do it by myself. I do this with the material that I'm fortunate enough to be loaned. You allow it to infect the audience the way it did when you first read it or first listened to it."

about the author

Lawrence Thelen is a director working primarily in the musical theatre. He holds degrees from U.S.C. and Washington State University. Originally from California, he resides in New Jersey with his wife, costume designer Irene V. Hatch.

index